THE FUNDRAISING SERIES

FUNDRAISING DATABASES

Peter Flory

GW00504616

The fundraising series

Community Fundraising Harry Brown

Corporate Fundraising Valerie Morton (editor)

Fundraising Databases Peter Flory

Fundraising Strategy Redmond Mullin

Legacy Fundraising Sebastian Wilberforce (editor)

Trust Fundraising Anthony Clay (editor)

Copyright © 2001 Directory of Social Change

The moral right of the author has been asserted in accordance with the Copyrights, Designs and Patents Act 1988.

Published by
The Directory of Social Change   Tel 020 7209 5151
24 Stephenson Way   Fax   020 7209 5049
London   e-mail: info@dsc.org.uk
NW1 2DP   from whom further copies and a
                               full publications list are available.

The Directory of Social Change is a Registered Charity no. 800517

Design and production Eugenie Dodd Typographics
Printed and bound by Bell & Bain Ltd, Glasgow

British Library Cataloguing in Publication Data
A catalogue record for this book is available from the British Library

ISBN 1 900360 91 8

Contents

Acknowledgements

The author wishes to thank Andrew Watt of ICFM for his helpful comments during the preparation of this book.

A special vote of thanks is due to the following people for sharing their experiences of fundraising databases:

Sharon Adams of Beating Bowel Cancer

Ann Bailey of The Pituitary Foundation

Claire Brooke of SANE

Sarah Burgess of the Royal National Lifeboat Institution

Dave Carlos of Care for the Family

Simon Cooper of Motor Neurone Disease Association

Phil Durbin of UNICEF

Jenny Jones of the Foundation of Lady Katherine Leveson

John Lister of Sight Savers International

Ros Wynne formerly of Breakthrough Breast Cancer

The author would also like to thank his wife Sandra for her proof-reading, helpful suggestions and for generally putting up with him while he was absorbed in this work.

The fundraising series

Fundraising is a profession in a constant state of evolution; to meet the challenge that this presents, fundraisers must also evolve. Fundraisers look to the future, anticipate need and develop new techniques to fulfil it. The DSC/CAF/ICFM fundraising series seeks to address the full range of fundraising activity and technique in one series.

Each successive volume addresses one key element in the full battery of fundraising skills. As the series develops, it will cover the broadest spectrum of fundraising experience currently available. Like fundraising itself, there is no finite limit to the series. As fields develop, so new titles will be added and old ones revised.

The titles are intended not as manuals or directories but as texts explaining and debating fundraising within a framework that derives from the workplace. These texts are to be written as well as used by academics and practitioners alike. Each title addresses the core competencies within the ICFM's Certificate of Fundraising Management, ensuring their relevance to working practice.

Each title aims to place the activity covered in the text within its historical, ethical and theoretical context, demonstrating its relationship to current practice. The main body of the text proceeds to analyse current activity and to identify the constituent areas needed to guide future strategy.

The ICFM is well situated to assist in the production of this series; without the support, assistance and expertise of its members and their colleagues, the continued development of the series would not be possible. I would like to thank all those who have contributed and are currently contributing to what continues to be the most comprehensive fundraising series available today.

Andrew Watt
Head of policy, ICFM

About the author

Peter Flory, BSc., CEng., MBCS, MIMgt., MICFM, is an independent Information Technology and business consultant. He has been in the computer industry since 1965, and has been a management consultant since 1981, specialising in charity and membership organisations since 1986. In 1989 he formed Athena Consultants to provide independent and ethical consultancy services to a wide range of clients. Since 1990 he has worked solely in the voluntary sector.

Peter's career in IT has encompassed programming, systems analysis, project management and IT management. As a consultant he has handled many projects for all types of businesses. He is a 'hands-on' technical specialist too, numbering several programming languages in his repertoire, and has experience in all the main operating systems and hardware platforms. He specialises in improving business efficiency through the effective use of technology.

Peter assists clients with the complete 'IT life-cycle' – IT strategy development, requirements specification, invitation to tender procedures, project management, quality assurance, implementation support and operational reviews. He runs seminars on IT strategy and on fundraising software and has written a book on fundraising databases for the smaller organisation.

Peter is a very active member of ICFM, including being the chairman of the IT Special Interest Group. He is dedicated to bridging the communications gap between fundraisers and IT people. He has designed fundraising databases himself, both large and small. He works with fundraisers, not only to specify their requirements and help them to choose the most appropriate database, but also to help them understand what is possible, what is practical and what they can expect from a fundraising database. This book is a distillation of his knowledge of fundraising databases gathered over the past 15 years.

Peter Flory can be contacted at Athena Consultants Limited on 0118 986 6623 or e-mail peterflory@compuserve.com

Preface

Fundraising is becoming ever more competitive and sophisticated. There are more non-profit organisations than ever before calling for people's spare cash. The public as a whole are becoming more sceptical and discerning. In short, fundraising is becoming more difficult. Consequently, fundraisers need all the help they can get to achieve their targets. This book deals with a tool that is essential to every fundraiser: the fundraising database. Used properly, this tool will assist fundraisers to achieve their targets, or at the very least, it will help them measure their progress towards their targets. The fundraiser needs to accumulate facts about hundreds, thousands, tens of thousands or even hundreds of thousands of people and organisations. These facts have to be recorded and manipulated. They have to be sorted. They have to be analysed, summarised and reviewed. They have to be linked together. Conclusions have to be drawn from them. They have to be used to help the organisation make money. They have to be turned into information that will help the organisation make even more money. Unless fundraisers are dealing with a very small number of supporters, say less than 100, they will need the help of modern technology. Technology automates long boring tasks. Technology helps you to be consistent. Technology can provide the information that enables you to make better decisions. In short, technology can help you, the fundraiser, to be more effective. This book helps by describing what a fundraising database can and should be able to do.

The audience for this book

This book will be of value to all fundraisers, irrespective of the area of fundraising in which they work. It covers the needs of direct marketing fundraisers, face-to-face fundraisers, trust fundraisers, corporate fundraisers, legacy fundraisers, community fundraisers, events organisers and trading managers. Information technology (IT) is considered by many fundraisers to be too difficult to understand and something to be steered away from. This is not the case. It can be understood by 'real' people. It just needs to be put into everyday language. You don't have to understand how the 'bits and bytes' work in order to know how to use it effectively. You do, however, need to understand exactly what can be achieved and what you should expect technology to do for you.

The book will also be of interest to IT people who want to know more about fundraising and the processes carried out by fundraisers. Too many IT people continue to live in 'ivory towers' and do not consider the needs of the people for whom they are designing the systems. To some extent this is understandable; you don't know exactly what is needed in order to do a job most effectively if you haven't actually tried to do that job yourself, and very few IT people have been fundraisers.

The structure of the book

The book starts with an introduction to what a database is, a brief history of fundraising databases and some technical issues of which the fundraiser needs to be aware. The book is then divided into three parts. Part 1 is entitled *Why do fundraisers need a database?* It contains a discussion of how a database can assist the fundraiser in every aspect of their work and an introduction to the many packaged fundraising databases that are available.

Part 2, *Constructing and using a fundraising database*, is the main body of the book. It follows the traditional fundraising cycle of Making the Case, Research, Strategy and Monitoring and shows how a database can help with every stage. Making the Case looks at how the database can help to manage and monitor campaigns and funds. The Research section starts with all the data that needs to be recorded about supporters of all types, be they individuals or organisations. It then considers how relationships between supporters are recorded. The section then examines the essential and often knotty problem of segmentation. This is an area of particular interest where the power of the modern computer can be used to great advantage. The Strategy section looks at use of the database related to the various ways of making approaches to existing and potential supporters: direct mail, personal contact, legacies, events, community fundraising and trading operations. The final subject covered in this section is 'customer care', which in the case of fundraising concerns the supporter. The Monitoring section looks at the processing and management of income of all types, including various committed giving schemes, Gift Aid and legacy administration. Part 2 concludes with some words on essential administrative functions related to databases, some non-fundraising but related database functions and the all important Data Protection Act.

Part 3, *Future directions*, looks at areas where the fundraising database is keeping pace with modern technology, particularly in relation to the Internet and online fundraising. It considers such questions as 'Is it possible and practical to have a single corporate database?' and discusses the possibility of linking one organisation's database to databases of other organisations. Part 3 concludes with the premise that fundraising databases are becoming increasingly complex and sophisticated in their operations but at the same time they are becoming increasingly easy to use.

Technical jargon and how to handle it

Jargon is kept to an absolute minimum throughout the book but the very nature of the subject means that it cannot be eliminated completely. It is important that fundraisers learn the meaning of some of the technical terms in order to communicate effectively with IT people who develop and maintain the database systems. A glossary is provided for those terms that are essential.

Introduction

This introduction begins by explaining the structure of a computerised database – its elements and what links them. It moves on to say that these elements and their links can perform certain functions and that these functions can be utilised to create, store, use and analyse data. The nature and use of databases specifically for fundraisers is then introduced, and a brief history of their development is given. The rest of the introduction concerns technology issues, and how to assess your organisation's requirements in this respect.

What is a database?

A database is a collection of related facts. It doesn't have to be held on a computer but when it is, it is held in a structured manner and has a Database Management System (DBMS) to allow the user to update it, query it and report on it. A DBMS has other functions such as managing the security and integrity of the data, but the user of the system is primarily interested in getting data into the system, changing it where necessary, looking at the data in different ways, and getting the data back out again usually in printed form.

The traditional way of describing the structure of a database is that a database consists of files, which in turn consist of records, which in turn consist of fields. An example of a field would be a postcode, which along with several other fields make up an address record. A record for your address along with the records for lots of other people's addresses makes up an address file. The address file along with files of other data items, makes up a database.

FIGURE 1 DATABASE STRUCTURE

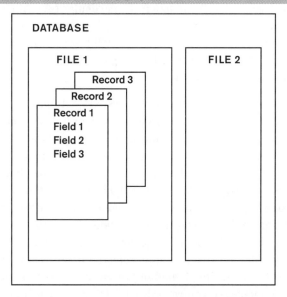

More recently, files, records and fields have been thought of as tables, rows and cells. Tables equate to files, rows equate to records and cells equate to fields – just think of a series of spreadsheets. The coming of the relational database precipitated this change in the way of describing things because computer systems could now access data by columns as well as rows (see Figure 2):

- accessing an address table by rows produces you every element of the address of one particular person

- accessing the address table by columns produces you a list of every single postcode in the table.

FIGURE 2 EXAMPLE OF A DATABASE TABLE

Column

Row

	A	B	C	D	E	F
1	Title	First Name	Last Name	Company	Postcode	Telephone No
2	Ms	Jane	Abernathy	The Training Shop	W1 1AA	020 7111 2222
3	Mr	Brian	Jones	ABC Holdings plc	EC2A 2BB	020 7123 4567
4	Mr	Paul	Jones	ABC Ltd	SL10 4XZ	01753 123 456
5	Mrs	Joanne	Longton	PQR plc	M6 2AB	0161 123 4567
6	Mr	Robin	Merrick	XYZ Ltd	EC2A 7QQ	020 7222 3333
7						
8						

Cell

Now you have tables (files), rows and columns (records) and cells (fields), where a cell is the junction of a particular row with a particular column, for example your postcode. The terms files and tables, records and rows, and, fields and cells will be used interchangeably throughout this book as you will hear people use both sets of terms when they talk about databases.

You need one further concept to understand databases, and that is the fact that individual tables can be related (or linked) to each other. For example, a table of people can be related to a table of gifts. One person can give you none, one or many gifts. It is difficult to maintain gift data in the same table as the individual's personal details because how many gifts do you allow for? The easiest way is to have both a table of personal information and a table of gifts for that person (see Figure 3). All you need to relate these tables together is something that is the same in the rows in each table. In this case, people and gifts, it is what is often referred to as a URN – a Unique Reference Number. This is nothing more than a shorthand way of identifying people, so you record the URN in its own column of the gift table rather than the full name and address.

FIGURE 3 EXAMPLE OF TWO LINKED TABLES

(This example is shown in the classic Microsoft Access relationships format.)

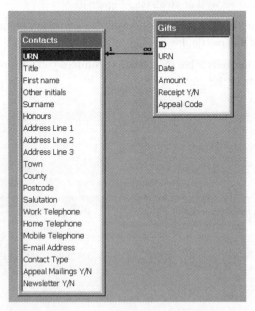

So now a database can be defined as a linked series of tables that serve a particular purpose.

What is a fundraising database?

It is simply a series of linked tables that pertain to fundraising, such as: names, addresses, gifts, legacies, appeals, funds and many more.

What is a fundraising database system?

It is a series of linked tables that pertain to fundraising along with the ability to carry out functions or operations related to fundraising, such as, producing personalised appeal letters, recording and analysing gift information and many, many more.

For the purposes of this book, the term 'fundraising database' will include the term 'fundraising database system'.

A brief history of fundraising databases

Thirty years ago there were no such things as fundraising databases. These were the days before PCs.

In the 1970s computers were large and expensive. Even a so-called mini-computer with five terminals would cost you £40,000. If charities wished to record details of supporters and their donations, their only options were as follows.

- To write their own systems (or have them written by a software house). This was very expensive and only the largest charities could afford it.

- To use a computer bureau. This became very popular. The system development costs were borne by the bureau who operated large mainframe computers (usually IBM) and who processed charities' income records. Each charity paid on a per transaction basis, so they had no large development costs. Later in the 1980s these bureaux began to develop communications links so that the charity could enter their own transactions if they wanted to. The biggest of these bureaux serving the voluntary sector was Southwark Computer Services who still exist today under their new name of Acxiom.

- To use manual recording methods. This was the preferred option for most charities, and involved manual record cards and hand calculations.

By the early 1980s a small number of packaged systems had appeared. CMG (Computer Management Group) and Minerva Computer Systems were early pioneers. Unfortunately, these systems were large, cumbersome and expensive such that they could only be afforded by the very big charities. At this time, 1981, the PC was beginning life, but it took a long time before fundraising packages were developed. However, a system called Donorbase did appear in 1983, and although it has long since disappeared, it really started a revolution. It cost much less than its predecessors and it brought fundraising systems within the reach of much smaller organisations.

All the systems of the 1970s and 1980s had a number of things in common. They were 'green screen' (because the screen was usually black with green characters displayed on it), character based (letters, digits and symbols – no pictures) and they were pure transaction processing systems. The emphasis was on automating the boring tasks of recording gifts and adding them up. The sophisticated analysis, donor profiling (see page 55) and segmentation (see page 66) that we take for granted today was not even a dream.

Then around 1990 everything changed. The PC had become widespread and many new products appeared that were developed for PC networks. They still had the look and feel of the old systems but they were a little more sophisticated, were easier to use and were usually under the control of the fundraisers (rather than the IT department) because they, and their associated hardware (the PC), were much more affordable.

The two major products to hit the market in 1990 were The Raiser's Edge and Alms. The Raiser's Edge arrived from the USA where it had been very successful for several years. It was very comprehensive with 40 main menu functions and at £6,000 was affordable to a huge number of charities. It was very rigid in the way that it worked but it did most of the things that fundraisers wanted it to do. It came with around 100 standard reports and it was like a breath of fresh air. It soon became very popular and its popularity continues to this day.

Alms was developed in the UK. It covered the same basic functional areas as The Raiser's Edge but it was designed to be very flexible and easily tailored to any voluntary organisation's needs. It too became popular. There were others but these two stood out above them all.

Then in the mid-1990s came the Windows phenomenon. The package suppliers had to redevelop their systems completely in order to take advantage of the new facilities. As the decade progressed the systems gradually became more and more sophisticated. Words like segmentation, Pareto analysis and RFV (Recency/Frequency/Value) became commonplace. We were moving from transaction processing systems to information processing systems.

And now in the new millennium the Internet revolution is upon us. Fundraising databases are becoming 'web-enabled'. This means that you can access your database from a PC anywhere in the country (or the world) via the Internet, and all for the cost of a local telephone call. You can even allow your supporters access to their records on the database, so they can change their own addresses!

Technology issues

Hardware

Moore's Law

In the mid-1960s Gordon Moore, who was one of the co-founders of the computer chip maker Intel, said that 'the number of transistors you can get on a chip is doubling approximately every eighteen months to twenty-four months'.

Technology is changing at a frightening pace. A new generation of computer equipment now arrives every 18 months or so; this means that the PC you purchased two years ago is considered to be out of date and in some cases the latest generation of database and other software systems might not work on it. It also means that a new PC similar to the one you bought two years ago can now be purchased for half the price you paid. Alternatively, for the same price as two years ago, you can now buy a PC that is twice as powerful, has twice the memory, has twice the disk storage capacity and has as many new features compared with the old one. When should you replace your hardware? How long will maintenance be available for your equipment?

Software

Moore's Law relates to hardware. A similar law could be put forward with regard to software; a new generation of application systems (such as fundraising databases) arrives approximately every three years. How long do you keep your database? Is your supplier keeping up with developments? How long will your database supplier keep supporting the version of the system that you use? Does it matter?

Operating environment

In addition to the continual changes in hardware and the applications software, there is the operating environment to consider. This is the basic software which allows the computer to function and carries out housekeeping functions such as copying files. Most of you will be familiar with Microsoft Windows, which is such a system. But firstly, there are many varieties of Windows. Secondly, there are alternative systems such as MAC-OS, Unix and the up and coming Linux. Which one is best? Which one do you choose? With your particular hardware, do you have a choice? Which one do the various fundraising databases run under? Does it matter? Should you be worrying about it?

Assessing your organisation's needs

The short answer to many of the questions above is 'Don't worry about it'. Leave it to the techies. The following guidelines are all you need.

- Identify your current equipment and your operating environment by answering the following questions: What is the specification of the PCs you currently have (memory or RAM is the most important item)? What operating system runs on the desktop and on the server (if you have a network)?

- Look for database systems that operate in your environment. Assuming you find some, do they fit your needs? If they do, then don't be too quick to keep up with the latest trends.

- If you can't find any systems that fit your needs, find out whether there are suitable systems that operate in a different environment. If so, then consider a change.

- If you identify one or more suitable systems, then try out their performances in a live situation. If the performance (i.e. the speed of operations) is adequate then don't change your hardware or operating system.

- If the performance is not acceptable, then consider a change.

- In all cases, identify your requirements of a database first and then carry out a cost–benefit analysis on the implementation of a database system. Remember, when doing the cost–benefit analysis, not all benefits have to equate to £ notes. Some benefits can be intangible and yet be of strategic importance to the organisation.

Why do fundraisers need a database?

CHAPTER ONE

Supporting the fundraising cycle

This chapter shows how technology exists to help you to achieve your objectives. Therefore, the fundraising database you choose must be selected because it will fit in with your wider action plan and help to facilitate your aims. It explains how the database can assist you in the four stages of the fundraising cycle, and that it should also be integrated with the organisation's overall IT strategy. It then discusses the importance of (and how to achieve) speed, efficiency and completeness in making the most effective use of the technology.

Every organisation has a mission that defines why it exists, whom it serves and what it does. From this it develops a set of objectives to achieve this mission. Technology must be the servant of your organisation and what it is trying to achieve. Too many organisations install the latest technology because it is 'the thing to do'. If you are going to install any technology at all it must be as part of an integrated action plan designed to achieve the major objectives of your organisation.

FIGURE 4 HOW TECHNOLOGY SUPPORTS THE AIMS OF THE ORGANISATION

When you plan to install or replace a fundraising database, you must know exactly why you want it and how it will help you achieve specified objectives. Your objectives must be clear and measurable, so that you can evaluate your progress towards achieving them.

DATABASE CASE STUDY CARE FOR THE FAMILY

It runs the 'business'!

In 1997 it was announced that Care for the Family was to become a separate charity from its founding organisation – Christian Action Research and Education (CARE). We'd known about this for the previous year and had already begun searching for the software infrastructure that would run this 'new' business, which already had 40,000 contacts and 15,000 donors.

We had just a few prejudices – sorry, 'reasoned positions' – relating to the database. Previous experience of bespoke systems, including CARE's, led us to conclude that we wanted a 'package' with full third-party support. Our 'one-database' strategy meant that we needed an integrated trading module. We also wanted a high degree of flexibility and customisable facilities.

After compiling a very detailed 'Invitation to Tender' we eventually chose Alms, the DOS version – Windows packages were still in beta testing and we didn't want to go through that particular process. We made one major concession as we chose the package – that we would re-engineer our business operations rather than seek to make bespoke programming changes to the system. We rationalised that any package used by 100 charities could 'teach' us and 'that different didn't mean poorer'.

Although a high degree of flexibility was a key specification, we weren't initially aware of the cost in time and staff involvement that this would bring. However, it wasn't all bad news – we really had to understand both our data and the direction we wanted to take it in, in order to bring the package into use.

Data conversion was a nightmare and a long lasting nightmare at that. Eight months were taken up in getting the data into shape and, inevitably, some mistakes still remain in the final data. Going live with the new software was three months late, data conversion being the main culprit, but a delay in finalisation of the trading module meant that we had to continue with manual systems even longer.

So what does the system do for us now, some five years later? The answer is quite simple – it runs the 'business'! Other than accounting and word processing, it is our central essential software system. We mail from it, we trade from it, we book holidays and we develop donors within it. One member of staff processes over 6,000 monthly payments, in less than two hours, using the bank's own data.

We take orders and information requests by phone, mail and e-mail straight into the system without paper records. We report daily on the progress of our appeals and projects. We send customised receipts to every donor, the content of each one differing, dependent upon the value of the gift, the reason for giving, the type of donor and whether we offered a donation incentive.

We currently have no plans to change, even to a Windows package, because they can't yet provide the functionality that we have in this system. It runs our 'business' – every day, every way, and it daily gives us the tools to enhance our relationship with our donors.

Dave Carlos – Senior Projects Manager, Care for the Family

IT strategy and the fundraising database

Fundraising campaigns will normally follow the four stages of the fundraising cycle as outlined in Figure 5.

FIGURE 5 THE FUNDRAISING CYCLE

- In 'Making the case' you are deciding what the appeal is all about and why you are doing it, what will happen if you don't do it, identifying the amount you need, and defining the benefits that will be derived from it.

- In 'Research' you are trying to understand the whole of your potential donor base and where support might come from for this campaign. You examine existing donors' giving history. You look at existing and potential donors and try to identify their ability to give, their capacity to give, and their willingness to give.

- In 'Strategy' you identify the types of approach you will make (personal, mail, insert, advertising, etc.) and the resources required (human, physical and financial). You then carry out the process of making the approaches.

- In 'Monitoring' you record the results of the approaches as they occur, monitor their progress, take corrective actions if necessary and if possible, and consolidate and analyse the income with reports, such as budget comparisons, return on investment, average gifts and patterns of giving.

Technology can assist the fundraising cycle in the following ways:

- During 'Making the case', you can analyse the results of previous campaigns that will provide data for your planning of the current campaign. You can compare and contrast previous campaigns' budgets, approaches, target audiences, responses and timescales with that planned for this campaign.

- During 'Research', if you maintain detailed records on supporters, you can make enquiries of the system to build up profiles of individual givers. You can segment the database in a variety of ways and on a variety of factors to obtain groups of supporters to target. This process can range from the very simple (e.g. who has given to this type of campaign before?) to the very complex (e.g. select all people who live in a particular area, who have expressed an interest in a particular aspect of your work, who are older than retirement age, who do not have a standing order or direct debit, who have given more than three times in the past two years, who have given at least one single gift in excess of £50, etc.).

- During 'Strategy', you can do mail merges to send out appeal letters yourself and record who you have approached and how. You can extract data (names and addresses) to send to mailing houses. You can create telephone lists for call centres and print detailed profiles for personal contacts.

- During 'Monitoring', you can record details of the income as it arrives and produce a variety of summaries and analyses. You can produce automatic, but personalised, thank-you letters quickly. You can record other information that is given to you by your supporters, such as change of address, what they think of you, when they want to hear from you and offers of non-monetary help. You can also record and monitor details of pledges of money.

To do all this you need a fundraising database, or more properly, a contact management / fundraising / marketing / banking / member-ship / subscriptions / events management / legacy administration / campaign management / fund management / mail order / sponsor-ship / grants management database.

A word of warning

Technology can assist the fundraiser at each stage of the fundraising cycle. However, a word of warning before you go headlong into choosing a fundraising database. Anything that you implement for fundraising must fit into an overall information technology strategy for the whole organisation. A prime example of this need for integration is the question of 'contact management'. As you will see in Part Two, many of the functions required of a fundraising database revolve around names and addresses and how you contact people. This functionality is relevant to all parts of the organisation and not just to fundraising. Therefore, it must not be considered in isolation, otherwise you are likely, as so many organisations have, to end up with several databases all doing the same thing.

Efficiency and effectiveness

The fundraiser who deals with many thousands of supporters and potential supporters could not do their job without a database on a computer. Drawing on the information in an effective database, the database system can search tens of thousands of records in a few seconds. The fundraiser who deals with a few corporate, trust or individual high value donors, for instance, can do their job more effectively if they have immediate access to all the information they possess about the particular supporter they are dealing with at that moment.

How fast?

Everyone knows that computers are fast, but how fast? What does fast mean in practical terms? Here is an example. All voluntary organisations carry out mailings. Let's say that you have a database of 100,000 names and addresses and you want to send a particular appeal letter to all people on the database who have given you more than £100 in the past, who do not contribute to you by standing order or direct debit, and who are interested in a particular aspect of your work. This is an example of simple selection criteria. However, you should bear in mind that it will take you several minutes to formulate the selection criteria into a question that the database system will understand.

The database will then be searched and all the people who meet your criteria will be identified and listed on screen in a couple of seconds. Another couple of seconds and the list has been stored away as a file that you can use in a mail merge operation.

Let us say that the database system identifies 5,000 people who meet your criteria. Now you want to print the letters. Firstly, you write your appeal letter. Then you carry out a mail merge operation. This can take from 2 to 20 minutes depending on the power of your computer. Finally, you want to print the letters. At the time of writing it is possible to buy an office laser printer, capable of printing 24 pages per minute, for less than £800 (including VAT). This means that a fundraiser can print 5,000 personalised appeal letters in a single morning. For much larger volumes you need more expensive and faster equipment and it is best to get specialist mailing houses to do it for you.

How efficient?

> **Mistakes on database records**
>
> Contrary to popular belief, computers do not make mistakes – people do. Remember GIGO – garbage in, garbage out. Also, computers never forget anything and they are always consistent. So, if you spell someone's name incorrectly when you enter it into your database, then it will be wrong on every single letter you send to that person.

Efficiency is in this context a measure of the effectiveness of the work carried out by the fundraiser. Using a fundraising database you can achieve a reduction in clerical work by the use of data entry techniques like generating the entire address from the postcode and defaulting the appeal code and payment method on batches of income items that are similar (see page 96). The system can then produce automatic thank-you letters for your donors. The system can also produce income summaries and income analyses in a variety of sequences and with a variety of different totalling. Typical examples are:

- today's income items in detail totalled by payment method
- this week's income items in detail totalled by appeal code
- the top 50 donations this week in order from the largest to the smallest.

Efficiency can be improved by using any of the following strategies available to the user of a fundraising database.

- Establishing a single database for the management and communication with all contacts of the organisation (fundraising and other), thus reducing duplication and ensuring the data is as up to date as possible because the first person to find out an item of information (e.g. a change of address) changes the database.

- Using postcode software to ensure that all addresses are accurate, thus reducing undeliverable mail and ensuring that more letters are delivered for the same cost.

- Minimising inappropriate mailings; if the database is used properly, all staff will know who is communicating with whom and why.

- Identifying and merging duplicate records, thus reducing duplicate mailings.

- Targeting appeal mailings more accurately by sophisticated selection and segmentation, leading to lower mailing costs and increased income.

- Implementing security measures to protect sensitive data from misuse.

When you purchase packaged fundraising databases you get tried and tested software with a minimum or errors, there is a wide knowledge base available (from the supplier and other users), and new recruits are therefore effective more quickly as they are using an industry standard system.

And how complete?

A fundraising database can store a complete picture of a supporter. As well as straightforward personal data such as name and address and a list of donations they have made, you can add:

- a list of mailings they have received so you can analyse what they respond to
- notes on other forms of support they are prepared to give
- mailing indicators (e.g. do not mail, mail only at Christmas, newsletter, annual report, etc.)
- their interests
- personal statistics (e.g. lifetime value, average gift value, etc.)
- links with other supporters (e.g. family, employer, etc.).

The key here is that your database provides a single source of information about each supporter/potential supporter, so that everyone in your organisation can see the complete picture even though they may only be dealing with a small part of it. A fundraising database can assist you to build up this complete picture by selecting records of people with important items missing (e.g. no title, no date of birth, no postcode) so that you can request this information from those supporters only.

The more information you have, the better will be your ability to profile supporters, segment the database and target specific groups with appeals that will obtain better responses.

DATABASE CASE STUDY
MOTOR NEURONE DISEASE ASSOCIATION

The Motor Neurone Disease Association is a national charity that exists to provide care and support to people affected by Motor Neurone Disease (MND), whilst funding research into causes, treatments and ultimately a cure.

The association has utilised a variety of database systems to manage key functions within the organisation. However, during the mid 1990s it was recognised that core data was being duplicated across multiple systems in different teams, to the extent that when a new branch officer was appointed, two computerised systems and three paper-based systems had to be updated.

A key decision was therefore made, to adopt and purchase a centralised database, which would meet a wide range of needs across the whole organisation. Although fundraising was to be a key element of the new system, something more than a pure fundraising system was required. We needed to track people with MND, supporters, members, branch officers, volunteers, different types of health and social care professionals, researchers . . . and hold specific information about each of these groups. We also recognised that any one of these contacts could potentially 'wear several different hats'. For example, a speech therapist might be a member, support us financially, and be a branch officer. Thus, it was important to be able to share this information across the organisation, whilst maintaining only one core contact record.

In 1995, after undertaking a formal tendering process, we purchased the DOS version of Alms from Westwood Forster. This was able to meet all our core fundraising requirements, including appeals, gift management, mailings etc. and provide us with the ability to set up our own specific data sets for managing the data that was unique to us.

Alms has the concept of 'groups' and 'interest groups' which enables users to create data tables that link back to the core contact record. For example, we created a 'group' for health professionals which allows us to flag health professionals, indicate the type of professional they are – neurologist, doctor, nurse, speech therapist, etc. – and record their potential interest in attending various events we organise. A 'group' for branches was also created to record the status of each branch, log their various meetings and activities, and provide links to each of the branch officers.

More recently, 'interest groups' have been effectively used to record information about equipment that is loaned to people with MND. This was previously a labour intensive, manual system, which required an individual's name and address to be written by hand at least eight times! Now the details are entered once on the database, with information about the equipment loaned – type, serial number, date requested, date delivered etc. Using templates and macros, the data is then pulled into Microsoft Word to produce various letters and documents.

There is no doubt that Alms has served us well during the last 5 years, and there are currently 80,000 contact records on the system, with 14 different 'groups' and 9 different 'interest groups' configured. However, we have recently reviewed our database needs in light of changing requirements, the need for additional functionality, growing data volumes, and improved usability, resulting in the purchase of Raiser's Edge v7. This is currently being installed and configured, and it is hoped to have everything up and running by autumn 2001.

Simon Cooper – Information Technology Manager, Motor Neurone Disease Association

CHAPTER TWO

Turning data into information

This chapter concerns how to extract useful information from the data in your database. It first describes the variety of formats this data can take and the types of fields you can create for them. It moves on to highlight considerations of how to access or search through this information, and then discusses methods of classifying your supporters by profiling their characteristics, and introduces the key process of segmentation to divide them into groups.

The people who develop databases almost always think of data and the structure of the data first, and the functions, or what you want to do with the data, second. Fundraisers, on the other hand, think first of what they want to do and only secondly about the information (i.e. the data) needed to do it. This has often led to problems in the past; a database has been designed, the major functions defined and then the fundraiser says 'I also want to do X' only to be told that it is extremely difficult or even impossible.

A recent system development called object orientation, where data and functions are considered together, should mean that this situation will become less common. However, having said this, the nature of your data and the way it is structured is very important and it is wise to give serious consideration to both before embarking on the development or purchase of a fundraising database.

The structure of data

Format

Data can be recorded on a database in a number of formats.

- Text – a text field can contain any alphabetic character, numeric digit or special character (e.g. / , £ (% + = – * & " @ ? #).

- Numeric – a numeric field can contain only numeric digits, but there are some forms of numeric fields into which you can type special characters and the system knows how to handle them (e.g. into a 'Currency' field you can enter £ + – and a decimal point).

- Date – date fields can contain the date in a variety of formats (e.g. 12/08/01 or 12Aug01 or 12 August 2001). Usually you can do calculations based on dates with the dates defined in any of these and other formats (e.g. to work out how old someone is or how long it is since they last gave you a donation), but beware; there are still systems around where you have to specify the date in year/month/day sequence (e.g. 2001Aug12) for this to work!

- Yes/No – a field that can have only two possible entries. They can be text (i.e. Yes or No) or a check box which is either blank or contains a tick (✓), or a 0 or 1.

- Table entry – this is a field where you can only enter a value (i.e. a number or some text) from a pre-defined list. Usually you can simply select the value you want from a 'drop-down list'. Once again, here is a word of warning: some systems have drop-down lists to select from but still allow you to enter other values. These values will not usually be stored back into the original table and so later analysis that you perform on the data may be incorrect.

FIGURE 6 EXAMPLE TABLE DEFINITION WITH DIFFERENT DATA TYPES

⊞ Donations : Table	
Field Name	Data Type
🔑▶ ID	AutoNumber
Contact Number	Number
Date	Date/Time
Amount	Currency
Campaign/Event Code	Text
Fund Code	Text
Receipt Y/N	Yes/No

Mandatory and optional fields

In addition to the format of the data, fields can be mandatory or optional. A mandatory field will insist that you enter a value before you can save the record. It is all too easy when entering new records to skip fields where you are not sure what to enter, in order just to get the basic record on file. A good way to ensure consistency is to have default values so that even if you don't specifically enter a value yourself, a value is inserted by the system. A simple procedure like having an 'Appeal Mailings Yes or No' field default to 'Yes' so that everyone gets appeals unless you deliberately exclude them is rather obvious (and saves data entry time), but using other less obvious defaults, such as 'Don't Know' for a Gender field, will aid consistency and analysis.

All of this may seem very obvious, so why do you need to worry about it? Here are some good reasons.

- Telephone numbers are numeric, but if you define them as numeric fields then you won't be able to enter spaces which make the number more readable nor enter a number followed by an 'x' or 'ext' and then an extension number. So Telephone number is a Text field.

- How do you create a meaningful analysis when a field in some records is 'Yes', in some records is 'No' and in some records it is blank?

- If you record gifts in kind (GIKs), you don't want the 'value' of the gift added into the value of real money donations, so most people, if they record it at all, put it in as part of a text field. But if you do that, how can you easily find out how much your GIKs are worth to your organisation? You need another Currency field for this purpose.

Accessing data

A major feature to consider once you have defined all the data you need to record, is how you want to access the data. Why? Because computers have ways to find things quickly and ways to find things slowly. If a field is defined as a key field or an indexed field (in Access terms – a primary key) then the computer can access the record(s) you want directly without searching through them all looking for fields which match your request, which on a database of 500,000 records could take 30 minutes or more. For example, you are looking up the details of someone named Smith; if the name and address table is indexed on Surname, then as soon as you press the Enter key to ask the system to search it will find the first Smith on the database and start to display the details of people named Smith. If, on the other hand, the Surname is not indexed, then the system will have to look at every record to see if it meets the criteria which can be a long process.

The key lesson to be learned here is to specify, at the beginning, the ways in which you want to search for records and have an immediate (well almost) response. Think of it as if someone was on the telephone wanting a quick response to a query. How would you find their details – by postcode, by surname, by first line of address, by bank account, by date they sent you a cheque, by bank account number, by CAF account number, by something else? Whatever you would use as a search key, then that field must be 'indexed' for maximum efficiency. You don't need to know how to do it but you need to inform your supplier what you want.

> **Accessing data on small databases**
>
> If you have a small database, say less than 5,000 records, then being clear about what you want to find on your database hardly matters; database systems like Access, for example, can find any given string of characters in any field in any record in the database in just four or five seconds.

Linking data records together

Related to the way that data is accessed, is the way that different tables are linked together. For efficient operations you must know what tables are linked to each other and how.

In one infamous case, a status report on deeds of covenant (thankfully now defunct) had to search 500,000 contact records for each of the 30,000 covenant records looking for the name of the taxpayer. The report took 12 hours to run!

Below is an example of a simple fundraising database with its table links shown. Some fundraising databases have as few as two linked tables and some have as many as 600 linked tables. Typical packaged fundraising databases have around 100 linked data tables. It is important to understand the basic concepts and how you are going to access and report on the data.

In the diagram below:

- Each box represents a table of related data items.
- Each solid line with a crow's foot at one end represents a logical link where there is a one-to-many relationship, for example one contact can have many gifts. (Note that one-to-many can include none, one or many subordinate records, e.g. gifts.)
- Each solid line without a crow's foot end represents a logical link between the tables where there is a 'one-to-one' relationship, i.e. a single record of one table is only ever linked to a single record of another table, for example content to individual.

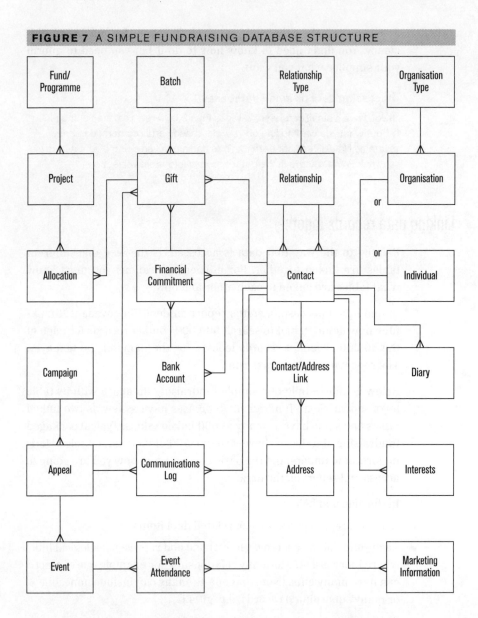

FIGURE 7 A SIMPLE FUNDRAISING DATABASE STRUCTURE

Obtaining data analysis and visual images

Thirty years ago when you entered details of gifts from your supporters into a computer system, you might expect to get a summary of gifts by income type or by appeal code, the next day. And that's about it!

These days, as you enter your gifts on your database, at the press of a button you can ask for an analysis of gifts by:

■ day

- payment method
- income type
- appeal code
- any combination of these designations.

You can see the data in numbers or in pictures. The figures can be seen in detail, in summary or in a variety of graphical forms such as bar charts or pie charts. Graphical representation should never be dismissed as unnecessary, showy and ephemeral. The old adage 'a picture is worth a thousand words' holds true. Trends and patterns hidden in columns of figures are immediately apparent in bar charts. A popular bar chart (see Figure 8 below) shows the total income for a specific appeal by day, that is a bar per day. This shows the pattern of gifts for an appeal; when they started to come in, how they built up, how they dropped off and how long they continued to come in for.

FIGURE 8 EXAMPLE APPEAL INCOME BY DAY

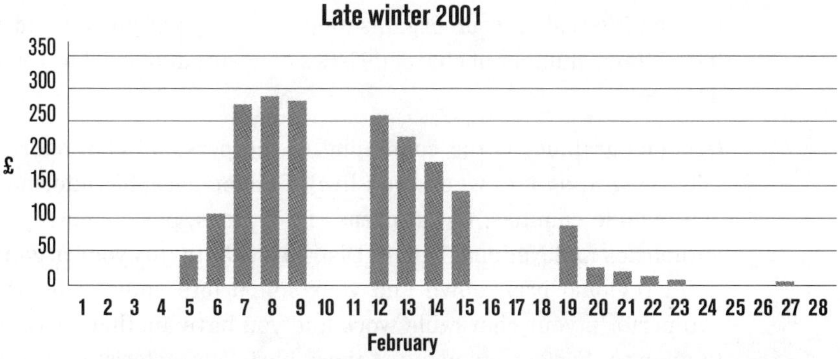

Late winter 2001

When you have bar charts for several campaigns you can use them to predict how you think things will go in proposed future campaigns. This graphical analysis can be taken to very high levels depending on how sophisticated you want to get (and how much time you want to spend doing it!). Other statistical analyses you might use include:

- scattergrams
- analysis of variance
- linear regression
- standard deviation
- chi-square analysis
- probability plots
- normal distribution
- Bernoulli distribution, Poisson distribution and many more.

(Better get yourself a statistician if you want to use many, or even any, of these distributions!)

On an individual supporter level, you can also immediately see individual donor statistics such as last gift, largest gift, smallest gift, average gift value, gifts this year, gifts last year or total gifts to-date.

All these things can be done immediately because of the power of modern computers and the ease of use of modern software.

Demographics and profiling

Demographics is the study of characteristics of people. As soon as you start to collect data about supporters, you can start to analyse their behaviour in order to approach them more effectively for future appeals. For example, you can record details of age, gender, marital status, denomination, occupation, home ownership, car ownership, income, children, leisure pursuits, and even information like which newspaper they read. Add to these pieces of data others that are of specific interest to your organisation (e.g. ways of giving) and you have a huge number of characteristics on your database that you can analyse.

Geodemographics is the combining of the personal characteristics with geography (i.e. where you live). Geodemographic information can include counties, postal areas, TV regions, parliamentary constituencies and National Health Districts. Add to this your organisation's regional breakdown and your supporters' interest in where you perform your charitable work and you have another set of data to analyse. Various elements of these basic characteristics are then combined together to form lifestyle indicators or profile codes for your supporters. The possible combinations of these characteristics are endless and you have to decide what is important to your organisation.

Luckily you don't have to start from scratch with all of this; specialist companies have developed ways of summarising the most important of your supporters' general characteristics into a small number of factors, comparing all the records on your database against their factors and consequently 'profiling' your data. This is all based on postcode. The most popular of these is the ACORN Classification Code from CACI (see Chapter 5, page 70 for a further discussion of demographics).

Segmentation and selections

Segmenting your database is simply dividing your supporters into groups. All supporters in one group have something in common with each other; at a low level it could be something like age or gender and at a high level it could be the ACORN Classification code. You may treat each group differently but you treat everyone in that group in the same way. For example you might divide supporters into several groups depending on the average value of the gifts they have given before. You then ask people with higher averages for higher amounts and people with lower averages for lower amounts.

There are three main ways of segmenting your database related to the money that supporters have given you in the past. These are:

- recency – when they last donated
- frequency – how often they have donated and value
- value – how much they have given you.

These segmentations can be used singly or in various combinations and Chapter 5 will discuss this in more detail.

The possibilities for segmentation are endless. Once you have segmented the database, you then carry out your selections, that is you choose the records you are going to do something with. The important thing to do is to select all the people in your chosen groups, communicate with them (e.g. mail them) and analyse the responses you get. You can then see where you need to put in extra effort to obtain better responses, or how you can change segments to obtain better responses or even analyse trends and predict how future campaigns will perform.

CHAPTER THREE

Packaged database systems

Despite the reduced flexibility of using a database system which you haven't constructed yourself, the many packaged systems discussed in this chapter provide a comprehensive variety of functions suited to differing budgets, sizes of organisations and scales of operations. This chapter presents the range of packaged systems on offer and considers their capabilities and costs.

It will surprise many people to know that there are more than 80 packaged systems on the market that claim to be fundraising databases. They range from 'shareware' (free) software to systems costing hundreds of thousands of pounds. They range from systems that consist of two linked tables (a name and address table plus a gifts table) to complex systems comprising over 800 linked tables. They are supplied by companies that range from one-man bands to those that employ many hundreds of staff. For simplicity the systems are categorised below as:

- very small – cheap single-user systems
- small – small networked systems, 2 to 5 users
- medium – medium-sized network systems, 5 to 25 users
- large – large networked systems, 25 or more users.

These divisions are somewhat arbitrary as some packages straddle the boundary between small and medium, and others between medium and large. Some package suppliers even claim to have solutions for every size of client from single user to more than 100 users. However, each supplier tends to do most of their business in just one of our categories. Where products are mentioned by name below they have been put into the category that represents the majority of their customers. Prices are given as at the time of writing.

Matching packaged system to organisation

Very small systems

These systems are generally limited in their functionality and operate on a stand-alone PC. Their functions are often restricted to
recording names and addresses in a single table, providing a simple
mail merge facility with Microsoft Word, recording income items and
a very few simple reports. The point about the names and addresses
in a single table is that if you have two (or more) individual supporters at the same address or one supporter has more than one address
then you are forced to create duplicate records.

This type of system is often adequate for a very small charity with little spare cash to spend on IT. They are a particularly good idea if this
is to be your first database system and you don't need to have more
than one person consulting the database at the same time. It is a
good idea to start small and simple and build up to a more fully functional system as you gain experience with the database and formulate your ideas as to how you want to use it.

Prices for these systems range from nothing for shareware systems
available from the Internet (or the basic one which comes free with
copies of Access) up to typically £500. They are definitely less than
£1,000.

Products in this category include Real Appeal, KISS Contacts and
Kubernesis.

VERY SMALL SYSTEMS DATABASE CASE STUDY
FOUNDATION OF LADY KATHERINE LEVESON

When I first joined The Foundation of Lady Katherine Leveson, a charity
providing residential and sheltered housing for the elderly, I had not
realised just how complex and diverse fundraising can be. Now, six months
later, I have come to realise that if you are to 'stay the course', you must
have endless patience, a memory like an elephant, innovative flair, sound
management ability and the capacity to work an 18-hour day!

As I started to deal with the many demands put upon me, I began to value
more and more the benefits of RealAppeal, a fundraising programme
designed to meet the needs of small charities. One of RealAppeal's
strengths is that anyone with basic IT skills can use it by following the
comprehensive, illustrated handbook. The package also comes with a
delightful tutorial and fictitious database, featuring Sherlock Holmes, which
enabled me to familiarise myself with the programme and learn the
rudiments of fundraising in a most enjoyable way.

RealAppeal is very inexpensive; the Basic Module can be purchased for
£250 and lays the foundation for the whole suite. It provides the tools

fundamental to the sound management and administration needs of most charities and enables you to: record, retrieve and monitor contact and company information; instantly view a detailed fundraising biography of each supporter; perform incisive and powerful mailshots; audit and classify donations; automatically print receipts; and design and store a register of documents and letters specific to your charity. An Events Module and Merchandising Module can be added at a later date, each at a cost of £200 and to complete the suite a Reports Module is available at a cost of £100.

I gather from Val Dub, an experienced fundraiser and my guru, that there is a need for a Fundraising Programme that does not baffle those lacking in specialist IT skills. In my view, this programme certainly fits the bill and is to be recommended to all those involved with fundraising in the smaller organisation.

Jenny Jones – Fundraising Secretary, Foundation of Lady Katherine Leveson

Small systems

There are many more systems in this bracket, which is designed to accommodate between two and five networked users. The majority of these systems are written in Microsoft Access or a similar development language. (Some of the suppliers in this group also provide a cut down version of their main product for single user use for around £500.) These are 'fully functional' systems that carry out most if not all of the functions that will be described in Part Two. Some of these systems can scale up to more than five networked users and still provide acceptable response times, but this should not be relied upon. Acceptable response times are subjective but some rules of thumb are: less than 30 seconds to start up the system in the morning, less than three seconds to find a single record after pressing the enter key and less than five minutes to carry out a selection of the whole database.

Prices for these systems range from £1,500 to £10,000.

Products in this category include AppealMaster, Campaign, Donorflex, Enterprise, Fundraiser, Proclaim, Subscriber, thankQ and Visible Results.

SMALL SYSTEMS DATABASE CASE STUDY
THE PITUITARY FOUNDATION

The Pituitary Foundation provides support and information to pituitary patients, their families, friends and carers; and works to raise public awareness of pituitary disease. Launched in 1994, we currently have more than 8,500 active members.

We initially used a simple membership database using DataEase. This worked very well for us for the first four years or so but, as we grew, we found we needed to hold more information about our members, as well as supporting our fundraising activity.

We planned a tailor-made Word-based database, and had initial discussions with a programmer. However, attendance at the Database 2000 conference quickly persuaded us that the bespoke route should be avoided at all costs. Instead we invited four companies to demonstrate their software; two were subsequently invited back for more detailed discussion; and we spoke to existing users of these two systems. A member of staff visited one of these customers where she was able to get a real feel for what the package could achieve.

We commissioned Subscriber in mid-July 2000 and were impressed that they took time to understand the workings of the foundation before amending their core package to meet our specific requirements. Installation and training took place in October 2000. Throughout the exercise, we did not lose sight of the fact that the database needed first and foremost to be a membership database, allowing us to hold considerable information about patients' medical condition, symptoms and medication, as well as supporting our fundraising activities.

In parallel with this project we also undertook a major Membership Survey with a 40% response rate. The two projects together have resulted in a sophisticated database which allows us to achieve the following:

- Quickly export information to our mailing house who handle our quarterly newsletter – previously we generated labels in-house which was time consuming and costly.
- Benefit from MailSort discounts on these mailings.
- Use PostCode Plus to ensure our postcodes are accurate.
- Undertake targeted mailings where appropriate.
- Administer our 'Telephone Buddies' scheme – whereby members provide peer-support to fellow patients and carers.
- Reclaim tax relief on covenants and GiftAid.
- Undertake statistical analysis of our membership which should result in a more efficient targeting of our services. It will also be invaluable in our search for funding.
- Benefit from telephone and online support.

The system is still very new and we are not yet using it to its full capacity. For example, we have yet to use the events module but as we stage a regular National Conference with more than 400 delegates, this will come into its own in time.

The project was achieved on time and to budget and I have no doubt that the database will prove to be an invaluable resource for us.

Ann Bailey – Manager, The Pituitary Foundation

Medium-sized systems

This is the category that contains the largest number of systems. The difference between these systems and those in the previous category is that these can often perform a wider range of functions and they are usually based on 'client/server' database engines such as Microsoft SQL Server. The client/server database systems carry out most of the processing work on the server rather than the workstation. This means that there is less data travelling up and down the network and the processing is being carried out on a more powerful computer. Consequently, client/server systems can handle larger databases and a larger number of users and still provide the same level of performance, such as the same speed of access to records and database selections carried out in the same time.

Prices for these systems range from £4,000 to £40,000.

Products in this category include C-MACS, CHAS, Pro2000, Progress, Raiser's Edge, smart, Stratum, Target and Visual Alms.

MEDIUM-SIZED SYSTEMS DATABASE CASE STUDY
BREAKTHROUGH BREAST CANCER

Breakthrough's decision to invest in a new fundraising contacts database arose out of the charity's first IT strategy. This tied in with a wider strategic review of the charity's activities, resulting in a new vision, mission and an ambitious target to double our fundraising income within five years.

We selected Raiser's Edge following a detailed tender process that involved all the fundraising managers.

A year down the line, we feel we made the right decision, but the implementation process has been lengthy and a lot of hard work. Having an adequate budget for the conversion project was critical. For example, we had to undertake a major upgrade of our network.

Users often have unrealistic expectations of the new system, as a database is only as good as the data that is put into it. Previously we had a main Access database and over 10 other ad hoc databases that duplicated some supporters. The data was often incomplete and of varying quality. Work needs to be done adding to and cleaning up contact details. However, we are already benefiting from a more coordinated approach towards our supporters.

The key process on the system is the logging and thanking of donors. The batch facility has allowed us to speed up data entry and improve accuracy as the fundraisers can view the batch before it is posted. The system now also handles direct debits and standing orders. However, the time savings were only reaped after an initial investment of time in setting them up.

We are investing in direct marketing for the first time to increase our regular donor base. Raiser's Edge has improved our ability to segment and target our supporters. Its user-friendly query writer and selection of standard reports allow fundraisers to extract their own information and gain a better understanding of our supporter base. The mail module allows users to do their own segmented mailing selections.

A downside of an off-the-shelf system is limited flexibility. We have had to devise some solutions that are not ideal, for example for our community fundraising appeal, the £1,000 Challenge. However, we can now benefit from the development resources of a large corporation and gain access to new technologies, like web-enabling. Greater flexibility will hopefully also become possible with future product upgrades.

Training is critical. Although the system is user friendly, we have found that staff need extensive in-house training and support, often on an individual basis, to apply its functionality to their particular roles. Fundraising staff turnover is high in the current market, putting pressure on our training resources. We have had to develop detailed written procedures to ensure ongoing consistency in the system's use.

The project has facilitated broader organisational change. The finance and fundraising teams now work more closely together, planning and prioritising activities through monthly meetings. The project has also encouraged greater coordination between fundraising teams, for example working on mailing planners and standard thank-you letters.

To sum up: don't expect a quick fix when you introduce a new database. There have been frustrations with speed and performance at times but Raiser's Edge is beginning to realise the benefits that we sought. However, there is still plenty of untapped potential because of the need for more time to be invested.

Ros Wynne – freelance consultant, formerly Director of Resources of Breakthrough Breast Cancer from March 1996 until January 2001.

Large systems

These are built on heavy duty (and expensive) database engines such as Oracle. They contain the same basic functionality as the medium systems, but the companies supplying them are also willing to tailor a system to the client's requirements. In other words, the suppliers of these systems make a significant proportion of their money from providing specialised additional services. They only suit the largest of charities, partly because these charities are the only ones who can afford them, but also because such charities are the most likely to have fixed or specialised ways of working that they want modelled in their computer systems.

Prices for these systems range from £30,000 to £300,000.

Products in this category include Charisma, Contacts Suite, Genesis, iMIS, MySoft, iMembership.

LARGE SYSTEMS DATABASE CASE STUDY
ROYAL NATIONAL LIFEBOAT INSTITUTION

The project was to replace our ten-year-old supporter system with a new relational database system. The new system had to run not only the donors and members, but also legacies, corporates, give as you earn and, ultimately, the regions.

It has been a long and complex process. Some things we got right first time, some we wished we'd done differently, but in the end we got what we wanted.

The benefits we have obtained from our implementation of Charisma are:

- Automatic fulfilment – All the receipts, letters and cards are there on the printer in the morning. It saves a huge amount of Supporter Services' time which would otherwise be spent manually requesting outputs or even writing ad hoc letters.

- Immediate reaction – Example: Not long after we went live, RNLI in-shore lifeboats were seen on TV helping flood victims in Sussex. Donations started to come in. All we had to do was to create a new source code, link it to some new letters in Word, and the automatic fulfilment module started to produce letters with specific text relating to our flood relief work. Our supporters were most impressed – and we had not asked Minerva how to do it.

- Income allocation – RNLI treatment of income is quite complex, particularly membership income where we differentiate between recruitment and retention income and break it down according to what stage renewal occurred at (renewal, first or second reminder, etc.). There are a lot of rules involved and users can't be expected to remember them all. The system now does it all for us and income allocation is fast and accurate.

- Easy operation – We specified a customer service help screen – a summary screen which shows everything we know about a supporter at a glance. Help Desk staff find this invaluable when dealing with a supporter over the phone – being well briefed about a supporter helps to ensure that their experience of dealing with us is a positive one. Difficult enquiries or complaints (we all get them!) are passed through to the Fundraising Director who uses the screen himself to build a picture of the supporter he is talking to.

- Marketing Analysis – Much of the design and implementation was carried out with our reporting needs in mind. We need to be able to see where our support comes from, what patterns there are in renewals and upgrades, and the relationship between legacy marketing and legacy income. The database design means that we can do this and we are now getting some really useful reports off the system without having to wade through mammoth listings, to compile statistics as used to happen.

A year after going live a number of follow up projects are under way, the most important of which is the regions. During the course of the project, the emphasis of regional fundraising has evolved in a way that means that we will be implementing systems differently from how they were originally envisaged. But then the systems must support the business and not the other way round.

Sarah Burgess – Supporter Services Manager, Royal National Lifeboat Institution

A note about costs

The prices quoted above are initial one-off licence costs. When you purchase a fundraising database you are actually purchasing a licence to use the system. You do not purchase the actual program code of the system and you cannot alter the basic functionality of the system. This means that the development of the system rests with the supplier. It also means that the further development of the system is tightly controlled and there are no problems upgrading to new versions as everyone is using the same system albeit in very different ways.

In every case there is an ongoing annual maintenance cost which gives you telephone support for the resolution of problems and which entitles you to receive new versions of the product as they are developed. The cost of this per year is between 15% and 20% of the initial licence fee.

The reasons why there are such large cost ranges quoted above are twofold. Firstly, different suppliers charge very different rates, and secondly, most suppliers charge a set price for the basic software (which can vary according to which modules you purchase) plus an amount for each concurrent user of the database. The number of concurrent users is the number of users who are actually using the system at the very same point in time. Before you buy a system you must be familiar with this concept of concurrent users. For example, you may have 20 people in total who want access to the database, but if only five people are going to be accessing the database at any one instant of time, then you want a five concurrent user licence.

In addition, if you are budgeting for a new system, remember that when you first implement the system, such things as training, project management and conversion of data out of your old system into the new one will be at least as much again as the licence costs.

Advantages of a packaged system

If you adopt a packaged fundraising database you can:

- take advantage of best practice by using a system that is designed to cater for the needs of the majority of the voluntary sector
- 'grow into' complex functionality that is already built into the product
- be reasonably assured that continuing support and advice is available

- be reasonably assured that the system will keep up with legislative changes and undergo continual improvement
- be assured that you have many to choose from
- be assured that whatever you choose is tried and tested.

DATABASE CASE STUDY **SANE**

Thanks to a Section 64 grant, SANE was given the opportunity to update its fundraising database in 1999. The existing database had a total of 30,000 records dating back to 1991. It was used to record all income, and also anyone who had ever expressed an interest in the organisation. It therefore included numerous duplicates, lapsed donors and 'gone aways'. The database was not very user friendly and because of all the changes in the fundraising team over the years much of the information it included had become meaningless and inaccessible. Also, producing reports was a long and complicated process generating limited information.

We agreed that a new database should:

- limit the possibility of producing duplicates
- be able to record the new gift aid
- have an easy way of producing financial reports
- be user friendly, requiring the minimum amount of training for users
- have room for growth
- have a good user support service
- transfer records across without scrambling any vital information.

The fundraising team saw presentations from three database suppliers. The first was rejected because it was a new product, introduced in 1999 and so the support was not tried and tested. Also the biggest database it supported at the time had 30,000 records and SANE expected their database to exceed this size in the near future. The team rejected the second product as it did not look good on screen, seemed difficult to use and the reporting method was complicated. It was also the most expensive option.

The team decided to select Donorflex as it looked easy to use, offered good support, was established in 1988 and had since been developed according to the demands of fundraisers.

From the start the Donorflex team were very helpful. Something that SANE hadn't considered was the process of transferring the data across from one database to another. Donorflex made the transition smoothly and quickly, consulting with the fundraisers at every stage and talking it through.

Two training days were included in the initial cost and once the team of three had been trained the system went live. Donorflex has proved to be an excellent choice. It meets all the criteria and makes it easy to do things that we would never have dreamt of on the old database. It is user friendly; entering duplicate records is almost impossible; it makes the new gift aid easy to manage; producing financial reports is straightforward with several options; the training was thorough; and the support team, who are available 9–5, five days a week, are helpful and patient, plus there is a user group. The names for fields are flexible so that we have been able to specify our own fields for entering donations.

Most of the hiccups that occurred in the early weeks were due to the muddled state of the data that came across, e.g. money attached to individuals rather than companies; a large number of records with out-of-date addresses; false donation history because of duplicate records.

The database is full of outdated addresses and cleaning it up will be a major task. Two mailings to the entire database generated a pile of 'gone aways' and helped to clean out the individual records. The trust and company records will take longer.

The result is that we can now segment the donors and target campaigns. The downside is that we now realise we have only a small number of real donors, with a lot of other addresses for people who no longer give. However, Donorflex has the capacity to build up our individual supporters with really accurate, up-to-date information which will facilitate real growth in this area.

Claire Brooke – Fundraising Manager, SANE

Alternatives to packaged systems

There are viable alternatives to packaged fundraising systems, one of which just might suit your organisation. Some organisations may not even need a database at all. Some people may have the skills to build their own database. Some may prefer to get a database developed especially for them. And still others may need a database but not the commitment of managing it, which can be a complex and time-consuming operation.

Manual operations

If you are a very small organisation with very few contacts, say less than 300, all of whom you know personally, then you may not need a database at all. You can quite easily operate with manual files, a diary/calendar system and a spreadsheet. Such an organisation is characterised by personal contacts, personal approaches, small numbers of large gifts and highly individualised communications. In these circumstances a database would be considered to be an unnecessary luxury.

DIY

The next stage up from manual operations is to build your own database. This option too is for the smaller organisation, one that does not have much money to spare for computer systems and one that is happy that their database operates on a single PC. It is easy to create a very simple fundraising database in a single day using Microsoft Access. Once upon a time it needed a computer specialist to develop a system, but now it is quite feasible for fundraisers to do it themselves. You only need either:

- a book that shows you how, or
- to spend £200 to £300 on an Access training course.

Building a Fundraising database on your PC shows you how to construct and use a database using Microsoft Office (see Appendix One for details).

However, there are a number of disadvantages to doing it yourself which must be pointed out:

- The one day mentioned above only gets you the basic tables to store the data you need and the forms to allow you to enter the data. It does not include the time required to develop queries and reports, which can be time-consuming and complex.
- You will need many different queries to create selection sets for different mailings (e.g. let's mail people who gave to us last year but not this year) and to provide selections of data for reports, (e.g. let's see how much the summer campaign has raised so far).
- There will be a temptation continually to 'tweak'/improve the system which can become a real time-waster.
- If you are not an experienced system designer then you run the risk of making a complete mess of your data if you are not very careful.
- There will be little or no documentation as to how the system was built, how it works or how it should be used.
- There will inevitably be one person in the organisation who knows and manipulates the database and when this person leaves, their knowledge goes with them.

DATABASE CASE STUDY **BEATING BOWEL CANCER**

Beating Bowel Cancer is a young and quite small charity. As with most small charities we do not have a lot of money to spend on computers and systems. Consequently, we survived for some time on simple procedures, minimal investment in equipment (often second-hand donated equipment) and systems that we often cobbled together. Our contacts database, or rather databases, grew on an ad-hoc basis and consisted of several Access systems and a number of Word mail-merge lists. What we needed was a 'proper' contacts database with all our names and addresses in one place.

We could not justify spending several thousand pounds on a packaged system, so we adopted the 'do it yourself with a little bit of help' approach. We had a basic management database created for us in Access. This database structure consists of just four main tables: contact names and addresses, donations, notes, and patient information. In addition, there are a series of list tables, five screens or forms and three income-monitoring reports. In order that we at the charity could take over the future development of the database, I went on a training course with Happy Computers in London to learn the basics of Access and how to write queries and reports. I now understand how the database has been built and I can continue to maintain it in the future.

Since my training I have been busy updating our contact list, from entering basic details such as name, address, telephone number, etc., to adding more detailed information of interest to us in any given entry. This has been a simple task to complete, as all I had to do was enter information as I went along, in the main table in the 'notes' category relevant to a specific individual, company, hospital or medical professional.

I have also found that I have needed to redefine some of the entry categories to be more specific in certain fields – for example, companies in particular – defining whether they give us money (sponsors) or we pay money to them (suppliers)!

One of the biggest benefits we have obtained from this new database is the ability to enter all donations received over the past year and, most importantly, the ability to record this information in more detail to show where the funds originated, e.g. a fundraising event, direct donation, grant, etc. This has been extremely useful in two ways. Firstly, I have been able to allocate and record the donation as restricted or unrestricted, and secondly, I have been able to view these results in a report.

Obviously, the most important benefit to everyone in the office is the fact that we now have all our contacts in one user-friendly programme on our PCs and everyone can access this information any time they need. We don't all have to rely on one card file system.

I have been creating queries to sort all this information into specific categories so I can run off reports that give myself and my colleagues a list of specific people, companies, events, etc. The benefit of this is that I can tailor the lists according to each person's requirements and what they need to get out of the database at any given time.

We shall be using the database extensively for Loud Tie Day, our major yearly awareness and fundraising event, to create mailshots, labels for mailing lists and to analyse the monies coming in from this, and other fundraising events.

Sharon Adams – Office Controller, Beating Bowel Cancer

Bespoke (Software house)

You can specify your needs regarding a database and its required functions and you can have the system developed especially for you by a firm of IT professionals who work for a software house. In this case the system will (or should) perform exactly the functions you want it to perform and perform them in exactly the way you want them performed. This will be very expensive initially and will take longer to develop than the time required to implement a package, but you should get exactly what you want in the end. With so many packaged systems available, the only reason to take the bespoke route is if a large number of your requirements are unique and not available in packages, which can sometimes be the case.

Bureaux/ASPs

The once popular idea of outsourcing your database to a computer bureau is making a comeback in the form of the ASP, the Application Service Provider. In this case the ASP holds your database on their computer and you access it from your PC via a telephone connection. You enter data on your PC which is sent down the wire to the database and you request reports which are produced on the ASP's computer and sent back down the wire for you to print out. Whether or not to consider outsourcing is often the subject of long debates within organisations. Many people are worried about losing control of their major organisational asset, their contact database, if they outsource. Certainly the database is held on a computer outside the organisation, sometimes as far away as the USA. However, it is accessible at any time via communication links, which is often via the Internet these days.

Other arguments against the use of ASPs are:

- They are too general in their operation and don't have your organisation's best interests at heart.
- They are too impersonal and don't have the detailed knowledge of the workings of your organisation nor the detailed knowledge of your supporters.
- The relationship with the supplier is difficult to manage.
- They are in it for the money.

Arguments in favour of ASPs include:

- They take the strain and cope with peaks and troughs in workload.
- You need less technical staff and can concentrate your resources on the business of fundraising.

- You need less investment in hardware.

- Cash flow is smoothed because there is no large initial investment, costs are more predictable and in some cases it can even be cheaper in the long term.

Which one is for you?

So when should you consider one of the above options rather than a packaged fundraising database, and which one?

Here are some rules of thumb:

- Manual operations – stick to manual methods if your organisation is very small, with less than 300 contacts/supporters.

- DIY – develop your own database in Access if you are a small organisation with 300 to 3,000 contacts/supporters and investment money is in short supply.

- Bespoke (software house) – have a database built for you if more than one third of your requirements are unique and cannot be satisfied by a package.

- Bureaux/ASPs – consider outsourcing if you want to minimise capital outlay and minimise investment in technical staff.

Constructing and using a fundraising database

CHAPTER FOUR

Making the case

The use of the database begins right from the start of the fundraising cycle with 'making the case'. This is where, amongst other things, you are deciding what the appeal is all about, how much you need to raise, your cost budgets, your timescales and your approaches. The database should provide facilities to analyse the results of previous campaigns that will supply you with data for planning the current campaign. You can compare and contrast previous campaigns' budgets, approaches, target audiences, responses and timescales with that planned for this campaign. There are two aspects to this in the database: Campaign or Appeal Management and Fund or Project Management.

Campaigns and funds

It is important to note the difference between campaigns and funds, and the database should deal with both.

- The campaign (or appeal) is how the money is raised.
- The fund (or project) is where the money will be used.

(In accounting terms these are known as Source and Destination of funds.)

In many systems the fund is defaulted from the campaign or appeal code, in other words the campaign is raising money for a particular purpose, so specifying the campaign in turn specifies the fund. This defaulting allows one fund to receive income from many campaigns, but it does not allow a campaign to raise money for many funds. This is fine for most cases because each campaign is usually targeted for a single cause, but it is more efficient to have complete flexibility.

Using campaign codes and fund codes

The other thing to consider is the structure of your campaign codes and fund codes. You need these to be structured in such a way that you can easily consolidate, compare and contrast the various campaigns you run and the funds you manage. The best arrangement is to have flexible matrix of codes but most systems provide you with a simple hierarchy of codes. It is typical to have three levels in each case, such as Campaign/Appeal/Segment and Fund/Project/Sub-project (see Figure 9 below). Unfortunately, many systems have no hierarchy at all, simply a single table of campaign codes and a single table of fund codes. The way these codes are structured is vital for easy analysis and comparison of one with the other.

FIGURE 9 A HIERARCHY OF CAMPAIGN CODES

Campaign	Appeal	Segment
New Building Campaign	First Mailing	Members
		Lapsed Members
		Reciprocal List
	Dinner	Tickets
		Raffle
		Sponsorship
	Second Mailing	Members
		Lapsed Members
		Reciprocal List
Care 2001	Inserts	Magazine 1
		Magazine 2
		Magazine 3
Support 2001		

Campaign management

What type of data do you need to record to support campaign management? As a minimum you need:

- campaign, appeal and segment codes and descriptions
- type of campaign
- income target
- number of approaches (number of people mailed, number of people telephoned, etc.)
- budgeted and actual costs

- start and end dates
- income value to-date (automatically updated by the system when income is entered)
- number of responses to-date (automatically updated by the system when income is entered).

With this data you can compare and contrast previous campaigns, and that will provide valuable summary information for planning new campaigns. Such information as overall campaign profitability (ROI – return on investment), cost per approach, cost per response, response rate (i.e. percentage response), average response value, are immediately available. At a lower level of detail, if you can 'drill down' from the campaign/appeal/segment records to see all the income items associated with them you can graph the income over the period of each campaign to see how the previous campaigns built up and tailed off. This information will also help with planning the current campaign.

Fund management

What type of data do you need to record to support fund management?

- Fund, project and sub-project codes and descriptions.
- Fund type (in particular whether it is restricted or unrestricted).
- Income target.
- Start and end dates.
- Total income value to-date (automatically updated by the system when income is entered).
- Income value to-date from each linked campaign (automatically updated by the system when income is entered).
- Amount spent to-date (probably manually entered although in theory it could come from a direct link with the Nominal Ledger system).

This data will help you to plan future campaigns to complete the funding required for your projects. Again, at a lower level of detail, you can graph the income for the fund and see its pattern. You can use information like this not only to help plan future fundraising campaigns but also:

- to plan when the targets for your projects are likely to be met
- to give the project funders an idea of the likely cash flow for the projects so they can plan expenditure accordingly.

CHAPTER FIVE

Research

Once you have planned a fundraising campaign you cannot approach potential donors until you know something about them, have recorded that information in your database and defined any known relationships between them. This is the most time-consuming part of the whole exercise, but arguably the most important. Data you record about people and organisations has to be accurate and up to date. You will record different data for different types of supporter/potential supporter and you will treat them differently. Supporters fall into two global groupings: individuals and organisations. However, within these two there are many sub-groupings, each with its own special needs. A key advantage of the database system is the ability it gives the user to group supporters by what connects them, such as their ages, locations and donation histories. The final section of this chapter looks at the ways you can segment your data.

Individuals – recording and relationships

Names and addresses

The storage of names and addresses is not quite the simple matter it may seem. There are several traps waiting for the unwary and you must take care not to fall into them: your contacts' first impressions of your organisation are important and you need to get their names and addresses right.

The following list details real-life problems with names and addresses, all of which have caused difficulties for various organisations:

- Not enough address lines, so the district, town or county is missed off the address.
- Blank lines on the address label.

- Inappropriate use of types of data, producing a letter addressed to 'Dear Electrical Limited'.

- Inattention to detail, allowing Sir Paul Jones' salutation to appear as 'Dear Sir Jones'.

- Inconsistencies in entering data, so for people living in North Yorkshire, some had 'North Yorkshire' under the county heading, some had 'N Yorkshire', some had 'N Yorks' and some had 'North Yorks'. This made it almost impossible to print a simple list of all the contacts living in North Yorkshire as no consistent search request could be given.

So what should you record?

- Name – with separate fields for the person's title, first name, other initials, surname and qualifications/honours.

- Alternate names – for instance, for celebrities.

- Salutations – both a formal and informal version, such as Dear Mrs Jones and Dear Pauline.

- Multiple addresses – each with separate fields for at least three lines of address plus town, county and postcode (and country if you have overseas supporters).

- Label/address name – for instances where you do not want to print the name as above in full on a label or envelope, such as Mrs P A Jones.

Using the Postcode Address File (PAF)

As accuracy is all-important, there are systems designed to link with most fundraising databases that help you maintain accurate addresses. These systems utilise the Royal Mail's Postcode Address File, commonly referred to as the PAF file (even though that does mean you use the word 'file' twice). There are many levels of these systems, but the basic level inserts the whole address into your database record when you enter simply the postcode and the house number. This not only ensures accuracy and consistency of addressing but it saves data entry time as well. Other levels of these systems allow:

- generation of the complete address from a partial address (useful when you have difficulty reading someone's writing);

- automatic insertion of parliamentary constituencies, National Health Districts, TV regions and other geographic breakdowns into contact records based on the postcode;

- regeneration of postcodes when the Royal Mail recodes an area – which they do all the time! (Note that if you don't do this then addresses that had correct postcodes when you entered them to the database may no longer be accurate.)

The most commonly used postcode systems that use the PAF are AFD Postcode, QuickAddress and GB Mailing. If you buy a packaged fundraising database, it will have links to one or more of these systems and your database supplier will help you to purchase and set up the system.

Recording general information

There is a huge range of information you might wish to store against people and many items are particular to your organisation. Some of the common ones are:

- major status indicators (e.g. deceased, gone away)
- first contact source code (how you first heard of this contact)
- date of first contact
- interest/support flags (one for every type of interest a contact might have, or for every type of support a contact might give to your organisation)
- gender
- date of birth
- occupation
- telephone numbers and e-mail addresses
- bank account and credit card details for standing orders, direct debits and credit card revolving authorities if you use any of these
- donation statistics such as donations to-date, donations this year, largest donation, smallest donation, average donation
- general notes.

Using category codes

Category codes are used for grouping similar types of people together (e.g. prospect, one-time giver, regular giver, legacy pledger). You may find that you need at least one table from which each supporter can only have a single value and another where each person can have multiple values.

The single value code table is to distinguish between supporters for whom you hold different types of data and/or with whom you communicate in different ways. Typical examples are: member, other individual, company, trust, church, school, club, branch of your charity.

The multi-value code table is distinguish between supporters who support you in different ways. Typical examples are: Gift Aid donor, non-Gift Aid donor, member, legacy pledger, volunteer, event attender, high value giver, etc.

Mailing indicators/flags

Mailing indicators/flags are used to determine who you contact and when you contact them. For example, some people are happy to receive any number of appeal mailings from you, whereas others may only want to receive an appeal mailing at Christmas. Note that you should ensure that they are all positive or all negative to avoid the confusion that could arise over such mailing indicators as 'No mail = Yes' and 'Christmas card = Yes'.

Although these indicators are primarily to control mailings so that people receive only the information they want to receive, it is common practice to include other types of contact indicators as well in the same set of data. This will include indications such as whether the person is happy to receive telephone calls or e-mails from you or whether you invite them to events.

Examples of mailing indicators could be:

- Appeal mailings   Yes/No
- Telephone   Yes/No
- Newsletter   Yes/No
- Annual report   Yes/No
- Raffle tickets   Yes/No
- Christmas card   Yes/No

You will need the information listed above for all the individuals with records on your database. The following types of individual may need specific information added to their records.

Volunteers

Volunteers or activists are special people who need special treatment. You may need to maintain details of:

- their areas of expertise
- their interests

- their availability
- where they will work
- training they have undertaken and when
- work they have done for you and when
- any incentives or awards you have given them
- any expenses they have been paid
- who manages them and when
- how they can be contacted.

High value donors and celebrities

These are very special people who must receive extra special treatment. They need to be excluded from standard appeal mailings and excluded from standard thank-you letters because they will always get personal appeals and personal thank-you letters. There will be a limited number of people in the organisation who can alter the database details for these people. Parts or even the whole of their records will be restricted access. For example, you may wish volunteers to know that celebrities exist on the database and you may even allow them to process income against these celebrities, but you may not want the volunteers to see the celebrities' addresses. The database should allow this.

You will have your own rules as to what constitutes a high value donor. In a small charity it might be anyone who makes a single gift of more than £100 or gives multiple gifts in one year that add up to more than £100, whereas in a large charity it might be anyone who makes a single gift of more than £1,000 or gives multiple gifts in one year that add up to more than £1,000. You must be able to specify the rules and the database must provide a facility for you to mark these people as high value donors. Ideally the system should do this automatically when the specified events occur, but typically systems provide batch facilities for you to run upon request. If you promote people to high value donor status then you must be able to demote them as well if, for example, they were promoted two years ago for giving more than £1,000 in a single year but in the last 12 months they have given only £50.

Parliamentarians, county and city councillors

If there is a strong campaigning element to the work your organisation does then you may want to record details of MPs and members of the House of Lords. If your organisation is small, you may be interested in the details of county and city councillors. In both cases, the data you might record about such people might include:

- political affiliation
- constituency
- their interests
- their voting records
- constituency office address
- secretary's name
- researchers' names.

You might also want to exclude these people from receiving standard appeal mailings and exclude them from getting standard thank-you letters if they make a donation.

Health and social care professionals

For many charities this is a group of people that need to be separately identified and given special treatment. You need to record:

- their qualifications
- their specialist work area
- who they work for (e.g. Health Authority)
- who they have helped (e.g. your beneficiaries)
- when, where and in what circumstances they can be contacted.

They might also need to be excluded from appeal mailings.

Media contacts

These are people you would wish to contact in order to promote your cause. Some non-profit organisations that make a great deal of use of the media generally use specialist systems such as Mediadisk (now called Waymaker Online) to maintain up-to-date details of these people. These systems contain details of thousands of named contacts in the press, radio and television at all levels: national, regional and local. Other non-profit organisations that make occasional use of media contacts keep their details on their main contacts database. If you are in this group, what do you need to record? A minimum set, along with the usual name, address, telephone and fax numbers and e-mail address would be:

- the organisation they work for
- the type of organisation

- the particular publication or programme they work for
- the type of correspondent/contact they are
- their interests/subject coverage
- their geographic coverage.

With this information to hand on your database, you are in a good position to target them effectively with your press releases.

Organisations – recording and relationships

One database or several?

There is a great temptation to have separate databases for different types of supporter, especially where different people in your organisation have responsibility for fundraising from different types of supporter, such as one for individuals, another for corporates and yet another for trusts. Having several databases should be avoided at all costs. Multiple databases will always have duplication. A trustee on the Trusts database may also be on the Individuals database as a donor. Ideally you want everyone who deals with a person or an organisation to be able to see the complete picture of your organisation's relationship with that person or organisation.

What you need is a single database that records information for all types of supporters and potential supporters. Much of the data you record will be the same no matter what type of supporter you are dealing with, such as name and address, donations and mailing histories. However, you also need to be able to identify the different types of supporters and record different information for each type, for example age and gender for individuals, industry classification and number of employees for companies.

Corporates

When fundraising from companies you need to know things about the company and about the people who work for the company (at least those who make the decisions about charitable giving).

So what information do you need to record about the company, in addition to its name and address? Useful items will include:

- its industry type (is its business compatible with your aims?)
- its annual turnover
- the number of employees

- the amount it gives to charity each year
- its giving policy (types of organisations/projects it supports and the maximum amount they give)
- to whom it has given in the past
- when approaches should be made
- how approaches should be made
- types of support other than straight cash donations that it gives (e.g. event sponsorship, gifts in kind, seconded staff, matched giving scheme).

Once you have the details of the company recorded you need the details of contacts at the company. The key elements are:

- name
- job title
- area of responsibility
- telephone (direct line if possible), fax number, e-mail address.

Note that these contacts might simply be company employees, or they might be individual supporters in their own right with a home address and personal details on your database as well. It is important to differentiate between the two different types of contacts. It is all too easy to send inappropriate communications when you have multiple addresses from which to choose. The individual only exists once on the database with a single personal details record but he/she is linked to more than one address so a clear indication of which address is which and used for which purpose is essential.

Trusts

Much of what applies to companies applies to trusts as well. You should record on your database details of:

- giving policy
- amount they give
- to whom they have given in the past
- when approaches should be made
- how approaches should be made
- the individual contacts (administrators) at the trust.

In addition, for the larger trusts there are usually fixed meeting dates that can be planned for in terms of preparing applications, and most importantly, there are the trustees. These are the decision makers that you have to convince, so the more you know about them the better.

Statutory bodies

Statutory bodies such as local councils and health authorities also have specific data items associated with them, if you have dealings with such bodies. Prime recording requirements here are the structure of the organisation (usually a list of departments) and who deals with what (a list of responsibilities). Both of these lists need to be searchable so that you can quickly find the appropriate person with whom to communicate.

Other supporter organisations

Other organisations that support your cause are many and various. They will range from voluntary groups with no formal structure to familiar organisations like Lions and Round Table clubs. The key requirement here, after the familiar one of having individual contacts linked to the organisations, is to be able to record items of data that are specific to that type of organisation.

Your own regions/branches

Many charities and other non-profit organisations have regional structures. Some even have two regional structures, one for fundraising and one for care/service provision. A typical structure is a three-tiered structure of Region, Area and Branch (or shop). Each of the entities at each of these levels will have post-holders, such as Chair, Secretary and Treasurer, and members. Members may pay to be members. They may not pay to be members. A single individual may hold more than one post. Post-holders and members may also be volunteers. Regions/Areas/Branches may have their own cost budgets and their own fundraising target. And then again they may be purely voluntary and have no targets. All these possibilities must be catered for by the database. If the Regions, Areas and Branches are entered onto the database as organisations in their own right then the following complication arises: 'What is the address of the Region/Area/Branch?' Is it the address of the Chair, the Secretary or whom?

> **The concept of 'nearest'**
> An interesting concept here is the concept of 'nearest'. A new
> contact/supporter on the database may want to know the location and

contact details of their nearest branch. Some of the postcode systems have the facility to automatically 'allocate' a contact to the appropriate Region/Area/Branch on the entry of the postcode. It is quite simple to add a table of Region/Area/Branch codes with a range of postcodes against each table entry. This is sometimes taken even further with the possibility for someone to be in two Branches (e.g. 'lives in' and 'works in') and even more sophisticated is the concept of 'nearest' by 'drive time' rather than miles as the crow flies.

Recording and reporting systems must be defined that allow income to be identified at the lowest tier of the structure and consolidated upwards (and not counted twice!). Political problems sometimes arise here when people in the Regions send money in to central campaigns. The concept of 'soft credits' (explained later in Chapter 7) in the database can help in this case.

Links and relationships between contacts

Every database contact should be defined (organisation or individual) and each should be linked to their:

- information records – such as mailing histories (for every mailing you have sent them), records of telephone conversations, meetings etc. (see Chapter 6)
- income records – when the contact/supporter has given you money (see Chapter 7)
- Gift Aid records, event records – and many more (see Chapter 7).

It is then absolutely crucial to link types of contact together. Three types of links are required:

- organisation to organisation
- individual to individual
- organisation to individual.

These links should all be considered together, viewed together and stored together. Beware of systems that have a multitude of ways of linking contact records together, requiring you to look at several screens in order to see all the possible relationships.

There are an enormous number of reasons to link records together. The following is a small sample to illustrate different types of links:

- a subsidiary company linked to its parent company, e.g. ABC Ltd (Subsidiary) – XYZ Ltd (Parent company);

- a daughter linked to her father, e.g. Mrs Pauline Jones (Daughter) – Mr John Smith (Father);

- an employee linked to their employing company, e.g. Mrs Pauline Jones (Employee) – ABC Ltd (Employer);

- a trustee linked to a trust, e.g. Mr Brian Jones (Trustee) – Jones Family Trust (Trust).

> **Reciprocation**
>
> An important concept here is that of reciprocation. This means that if you define Pauline Jones to be John Smith's daughter, then John Smith's record is automatically updated to show that he is Pauline Jones' father.
>
> There are still some systems, however, that make it possible to create one-way links only, so for example if you look at Pauline Jones' record and click a Relationships tab you see a link to John Smith. If you then look at John Smith's record and click the Relationships tab you will not see a link to Pauline Jones. Such systems are to be avoided.

There are a number of important system facilities to do with linking relationships, including the following.

- A contact must be able to have an unlimited number of relationships of an unlimited number of types.

- When looking at a contact's record you must be able to see, on a single screen, all the relationships that contact has, no matter what their type.

- You must be able to see the relationships in a tree structure (see Figure 10 below).

- You must be able to scroll down the list of related contact records and switch to viewing a related contact (e.g. you view the Relationships tab of Pauline Jones' record, you highlight the entry ABC Ltd (Employer), double click and you are now looking at the Relationships tab of ABC Ltd's record, so that you can immediately see other people and organisations related to ABC Ltd. With a single click you can then return to the main ABC record showing its address and other basic data. You can also return to Pauline Jones' record or move on to the record of someone else related to ABC Ltd.

- You must be able to allocate 'to' and 'from' dates to relationships. This is useful for defining committee membership or a contact's career progression. For example you can see not only who are the current members of a committee but also who used to be members of the committee and when they were members.

FIGURE 10 RELATIONSHIP TREE DIAGRAM

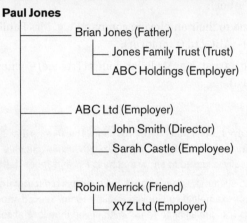

Paul Jones
- Brian Jones (Father)
  - Jones Family Trust (Trust)
  - ABC Holdings (Employer)
- ABC Ltd (Employer)
  - John Smith (Director)
  - Sarah Castle (Employee)
- Robin Merrick (Friend)
  - XYZ Ltd (Employer)

Using segmentation

Once you have recorded all the data you can about your contacts you will want to group them together in a variety of ways in order to make campaign/appeal approaches. The purpose of the grouping is to bring together contacts with similar characteristics, or contacts who may not have similar characteristics but who you want to consider and approach in the same way. The process is called segmentation, and this section of the chapter deals with:

- segmentation of the database based on simple criteria
- segmentation based on what supporters have given in the past (their donation history)
- segmentation based on characteristics that contacts/supporters have in common (e.g. geography and demography).
- the process of selection and de-duplication of the segments once you have identified them.

At that point you will be in a position to begin making your campaign approaches.

Simple segmentation

There are numerous ways that you can group your contacts together and you will have to choose the ways that suit you best. You might want to send different appeals to:

- people who pay by direct debit or standing order from those who pay by cheque, or

- people who have a current Gift Aid Declaration from those that do not, or

- men and to women, or

- people who attend events from those who have never attended an event, or

- people who have specified an interest in different aspects of your work or different projects, or

- people who have never donated from those who have donated, or

- people who have donated last year but not this year (identified by a LYBUNT report, Last Year But Unfortunately Not This) from people who have donated sometime in the past but not last year nor this year (identified by a SYBUNT report, Some Year But Unfortunately Not This).

Segmentation based on past donation history

Based on the principle that your most profitable future donor is an existing donor, most of you will want to differentiate people by:

- A breakdown (Pareto analysis) of your best donors (according to their total gifts to-date), your next best donors, etc. (see below).

- When they last gave, how often they have given or how much they have given (Recency, Frequency, Value or RFV, see below on page 68). Note that some people say RFM – Recency, Frequency, Monetary value.

Pareto analysis

This is the 80:20 rule of business; the principle that 80 per cent of income comes from 20 per cent of customers. In the case of fundraising, your customers are your supporters.

Most database systems can now do this type of analysis. They rank every donor by the total value of all their gifts since you acquired them on your database and then split the donors into decile bands. That means the top 10%, the second 10% down to the bottom 10%. Figure 11 shows a typical Pareto graph for a charity. The percentages will be different for each organisation (one charity that concentrates on big gift fundraising quotes 95:5 rather than 80:20) but the principle remains the same in that you can segment your database into groups of people who are worth similar amounts to you. Once an analysis has been created, the better database systems will allow you to link back to the contacts that are in each decile band allowing you to treat each band separately. For example, you could send one type of mailing to the top 10% of your donors and a different mailing to the bottom 10% (and all bands in between).

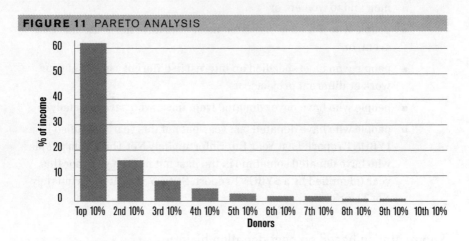

FIGURE 11 PARETO ANALYSIS

Recency/Frequency/Value

This is a much more flexible tool than the Pareto analysis and most fundraising databases can now go a long way towards providing all the facilities listed below. Firstly, it allocates donors to a number of bands (usually five) depending on the date of their last donation (Recency). You can choose the time intervals.

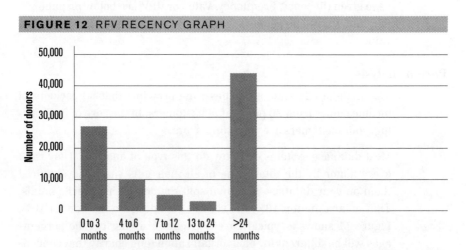

FIGURE 12 RFV RECENCY GRAPH

Secondly, it allocates donors to a number of bands depending how many times they have given to you (Frequency). Note that this is not the number of times in a given period as you might expect from the word frequency, but the total number of donations received. Again, you can choose width of each band.

FIGURE 13 RFV FREQUENCY GRAPH

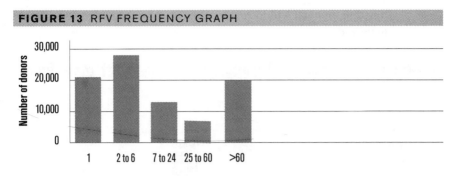

Thirdly, it allocates donors to a number of bands according to the total value of their gifts to-date (Value). Again, you can choose the width of each band.

FIGURE 14 RFV VALUE GRAPH

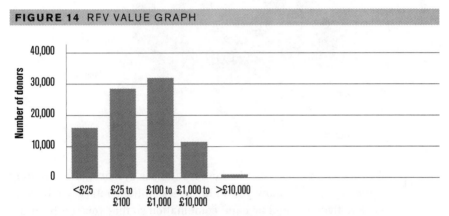

'Scores' are allocated to each recency band, each frequency band and each value band so that every donor ends up with three scores which are often added together to give a total RFV value. This is an advance on Pareto analysis, which simply looked at total value, because in the case of RFV you could find that a donor who gave 'little-and-often' ends up with a higher score than the person who has given one single large donation. You can tailor the width of the bands and the scores in order to decide which supporters are worth the most to you.

Once supporters are allocated to a band in each of the designations recency, frequency and value, you can examine combinations of recency, frequency and value (e.g. recency and frequency; recency and value; frequency and value). See Figure 15 for an example of one combination. Note that this gives you 25 blocks or segments of data to examine. If you can cope with the concept of data in three dimensions, then you can consider recency, frequency and value all together, but you will have 125 separate blocks or segments of data to look at!

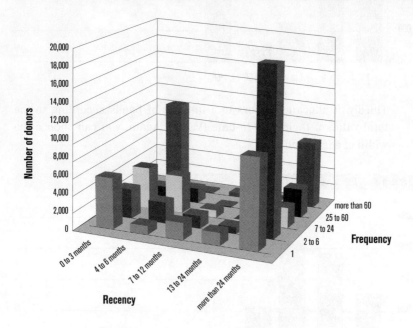

As with Pareto analysis, the better database systems, after creating the analysis, will allow you to link back to the contacts that are in each individual band or band combination so that you can treat the supporters in each one separately.

Segmentation based on demographics

Another way of grouping contacts/supporters is by where they live and by their personal characteristics. Geography is easy. You can segment by postcode area, by county, by health authority area, by parliamentary constituency, by local radio broadcast area and even by a given number of miles from a specified point (used for such causes as environmental disasters).

Demography is also easy once you have the data. Obtaining the data is not so easy. You may wish to segment by age band because you know that people of different ages respond to different types of appeal, but how many people will give you their date of birth if you ask for it in a mailing? Eliciting information about socio-economic group, denomination, salary, marital status, number and ages of children, all of which are useful in constructing highly targeted appeals, presents similar difficulties.

Some interesting help is available in this area from specialist marketing agencies. You can send your database to them to be 'profiled'. They will analyse your database (mostly they will match your contacts' postcodes with large tables they maintain) and give you back one or more codes attached to every contact record.

The ACORN Classification Code

This popular code was created and is supplied by CACI Limited. It gives you an indication of a contact's likely socio-economic status based on where they live. You get an idea as to whether the contact lives in a wealthy or poor area, whether they are likely to be young or old and many other lifestyle indicators. This helps you to target particular groups of people. It is important to remember that this is not an exact science. It is all based on averages so don't be surprised if you get a few odd results.

The ACORN code is a two-level coding system that classifies the whole population of the UK into one of 17 'Groups' (numbered 1 to 17) and one of 54 'Types' (numbered 1 to 54). Each Group contains two or more Types. For example Group 1 designated 'Wealthy Achievers, Suburban Areas' contains Types 1 (Wealthy suburbs, large detached houses), 2 (Villages and wealthy commuters), 3 (Mature affluent home owning areas), 4 (Affluent suburbs, older families) and 5 (Mature, well-off suburbs).

There are a number of similar-style profiling systems supplied by other marketing consultancies. There are also other types of profiling systems available where you can, for example, get an indication of the likely level of total income of every address on your database or you can get an indication of the likely age range of your contacts depending on a combination of their first/given/Christian name and where they live!

Selections and de-duplication

The words segmentation and selection are often used interchangeably, but there is a difference. The difference is simply that several segments can be combined to form a selection that is used for a single approach (e.g. a single mailing). Any particular contact record can appear in several segments but will only appear once in a selection.

The process of making selections can be very complex. Here are some functions that a selection system in a fundraising database must be able to perform.

- Allow the user to specify criteria to be applied to *any* field on the database and use full Boolean logic (ands, ors, nots, brackets and mathematical and text operators) on them.

- Make a count of records that would have been selected using the specified criteria without actually selecting or marking the records.

- Select on partial fields (e.g. the outbound part of the postcode).

- Make dynamic selections (i.e. the records that fit the criteria NOW) or selections fixed in time (i.e. selected records are tagged so that at a future date you can run the selection again and come up with exactly the same number of records). Selections fixed in time is useful when getting a fixed number of mailing packs printed. When the packs arrive you can run the selection again and get the exact number of records selected, even if the number of records that now fit the specified selection criteria has changed.

- Specify selections on the basis of *inclusions* (i.e. include records that match given criteria) AND *exclusions* (i.e. exclude records that match given criteria).

- Split selections into a specified number of segments of equal size or specified sizes (e.g. for sending out different mailing packs to people who all satisfy the same criteria).

- Hold and apply suppression files (e.g. run the selected records against the Mailing Preference Service file to exclude people who have registered with this service).

- Make iterative selections (i.e. a selection within a selection).

- Define a hierarchy of selections which are mutually exclusive. For example you might want to send Mailing Pack A to all people who have donated in the last 12 months, but you want to send Mailing Pack B to all people marked as high value donors (some of which will have donated in the last 12 months and some of which will not). The mutually exclusive selection stops people from receiving two mailing packs.

- Define manual selection sets (i.e. select contacts one at a time and mark them as belonging to a particular selection).

- Scroll through a list of selected records and manually delete records from the selection list.

- Make a sub-selection on a 1-in-N basis in order, for example, to do a test mailing and at a later date roll out the rest of the original selection.

- Specify one mailing per household so that that even if there are several individual supporters living at the same address then they get just the one mailing (e.g. useful for mail order catalogues).

- Define *standard* selections that can be run many times without redefining the criteria.

- Define *regular* selections that have parameters that can be changed at runtime (e.g. dates).

- Automatically include *sleeper (or seed)* records into every selection to check your own mailings. The seeds (often members of staff) can then keep a track of when mailings were sent out and when they were received, and that the right inserts were included. This is particularly useful in monitoring the performance of a mailing house.

- Automatically include dummy records into every selection for reciprocal mailings to check that the receiving organisation obeys the rules and doesn't use the list more than once or pass it on to anyone else. The easiest way to do this is to include a record with every reciprocal list that is your own name and address with your name spelt incorrectly. If you receive more than one mailing with your name spelt in this way then you know that someone is not playing the game!

- Ensure that records are not included in a single selection set more than once even if they fit multiple criteria.

Buying and swapping lists

Everyone wants to add new names to their database. This is easy when you conduct insert or advertising campaigns. You simply add new names as and when people respond.

The other way to add new names is one that requires special functions in your database: buying in and swapping lists. If you buy a list then the database must have an import routine to read through the supplied file and add new records, checking for and reporting on possible duplicates.

Swapping lists with other organisations, or reciprocal mailings as they are better known, are more complicated. Firstly, you have to select a set of contacts from your database that meet criteria agreed with your counterpart organisation. Then you have to mark these records as being swapped. And, finally you have to output the names and addresses in an agreed format for the other organisation – straightforward so far.

Note that you must now beware of the Data Protection Act, which is the subject of Chapter 10. You need people's agreement that you can pass their name on to a third party.

The problems arise when you come to use the names you receive in exchange. Firstly, you are only allowed to mail them once and you are not allowed to add any of them to your database unless they respond to this one mailing. But you need to compare them against your database because you don't want to mail any contact that you might already have details for. Your database system must have the facility to perform this comparison automatically and produce a mailing from the swapped list (without adding it to the database) while excluding any duplicate contacts.

Your database needs the facility to carry out complex selections, mark the records it has selected and produce a file of names and addresses in the format (normally Excel spreadsheet or CSV (Comma Separated Values)) required by your counterpart organisation.

CHAPTER SIX

Strategy

Once you have made your case and researched your potential donors, you will be ready to use the information to make approaches. These approaches could be by mail, personal contacts (such as a telephone campaign), running an event, or any number of community fundraising activities such as collection boxes, house-to-house collections, raffles or trading operations (such as selling Christmas cards). The database is required to manage and monitor these actions. The main output of your research phase is a series of selections, but what do you do with them? This chapter discusses the variety of ways to use your information through the functions your database can provide, showing how you can make effective approaches and responses to your contacts.

Making approaches by direct mail

The main thing that you are likely to do with your selections is mail the contacts you have selected. This section of Chapter 6 deals with:

- the processes required before you actually do the mailing
- the process of turning the selections into mailings
- what you do once the mailing has been produced.

Faxes and e-mails are included in the term direct mail. They are simply a different output medium.

Preparing for the mailing

What do you want to produce from your selection? Is it a file for a mailing house who will do the mailing for you? Is it mailing labels? Is it personalised letters? Is it donation forms/coupons? Is it a list for a telesales agency? Is it several of these things? Whatever the answer, your database system must be able to oblige.

Files for mailing houses are easy. Most fundraising systems can output data in one or more industry standard formats, the most common being Comma Separated Values (CSV). Also, most mailing houses are capable of accepting almost any format your system can produce. The only thing you really have to worry about is, if you are mailing multiple segments with different information, that you carefully label each separate file so that everyone gets the information you planned they should get.

If you are printing your own labels, letters or forms you need a facility to produce the label format, the standard letter or the basic form. Some database systems have inbuilt facilities for this but these systems should be avoided if at all possible because they are usually inferior to standard word processing systems, such as Microsoft Word, and you and your staff will already be familiar with Word from day-to-day work. So you should be able to set up labels, letters and forms in Word and your database should integrate with Word and not have its own duplicate facilities.

Sequencing the selection file

An important preparatory facility provided by the database is sequencing the selection file: your database system must be able to sort the file in any sequence that you define. You might want it sequenced in alphabetical order to aid visual checking and control of where you are up to when you (or your volunteers) are stuffing the envelopes. You might want it sequenced in contact reference number order for easy management. You might want it sequenced in Mailsort order (if it is a mailing of more than 4,000) so that you can obtain postal discounts. Note that mailing houses can 'mailsort' your file for you at an additional charge but if the database can do it then it saves you money. A complete Mailsort facility in the database will not only sort the selection file but will also print the appropriate bag labels and reports.

Turning selections into mailings

Once you have your standard letter/s or label formats prepared, you want to produce the letters, labels or forms from your selections. At the click of a couple of buttons you should be able to select the label format, standard letter or donation form you want and expect the system to do a mail merge. It may use Word's mail merge facility or its own. You and your staff will already be familiar with Word, so this type of system is preferable. The system must be able to insert database fields into the documents as per any normal mail merge. And it is not just names and addresses you want either. It should be able to insert information like suggested donation amounts that differ for each contact depending upon what they have given before, or different paragraphs depending upon interest codes stored on the contact records.

Merging information onto documents

The possibilities here are limited only by your imagination and by the way that the data has been structured; the flexibility of a system in this area has to be a key factor in your decision to buy it. The more your system will do, and the easier it is for you to set it up, the less time you will have to spend preparing your campaign approaches.

Faxes and e-mails

It is similar with bulk faxes and bulk e-mails. Your database should be capable of integrating with whatever facility you use for these purposes in your day-to-day work. For example it might be a system like Winfax for faxes and Microsoft Exchange for e-mails. As long as you are using something relatively well known this should not be a problem. To the database it is simply a case of outputting different data (e.g. e-mail addresses instead of mailing addresses) in a different format.

Mailing history record

It should be an automatic function of the database system, when you create the mailing, also to create a mailing history record for every contact that has been targeted. This is a simple record that need contain nothing more than the date, the campaign/appeal/segment code (or source code as you may call it) and the type of approach made (e.g. direct mail, e-mail or fax). Using these mailing history records along with the income records you create for donations that people make, you can analyse what people respond to and how often they respond compared with how many times they are asked (see Chapter 5).

There should also be an option to print a complete list of the contacts that were selected and mailed if required. You wouldn't want to do this for mailings of hundreds of thousands but for small mailings with many segments it can be a useful reference.

With every mailing you carry out you will always get some items returned to you for a whole variety of reasons, the most common of which being 'gone away'. It is important that you deal with these immediately by deleting them from your database in order to minimise wasted postage costs in future mailing campaigns. (Or you may simply want to mark them as 'gone away' so that you still have all their details should you at a later date find out their new address.)

Making approaches by personal contact

This section on strategy discusses:

- how selections from the database can assist personal (face-to-face) fundraising
- the recording of all types of communications you have with contacts/supporters
- the use of diary facilities for planning future approaches
- the recording and following up of pledges of help (both financial and non-financial)
- ownership and security issues related to the people you approach personally.

Note that the face-to-face fundraising referred to here is personal contact to known, or known of, individuals and is not the impersonal public face-to-face fundraising in the street referred to by some people as 'in-your-face fundraising'.

How selections help

Segmentation and selections create groups of records that you wish to treat in a similar way. A simple selection might have produced a list of people who gave large amounts in previous years but from whom you have heard nothing this year. A listing of these people with their telephone numbers backed up by a printout of all their relevant details could act as a programme for a telephone campaign. Similarly, telephone lists of all people who have been sent Gift Aid Declaration forms but have not returned them could form the basis of a telephone campaign that is outsourced to a telephone agency. These are simple examples, but they all start with selections.

Notepads: making a record of communications

If you contact people by telephone, fax or e-mail or if you have face-to-face meetings with them, then you must record the relevant details of the communications from you to them and their response. If you do this, then when you contact them again you start from a position of strength because, before you meet, with a few clicks of a computer mouse, you can see the whole history of the relationship. What do you record? Is it simply a case of an unlimited notepad? Unstructured notepads are almost (but not completely) useless. What you need is the facility to record notes that are structured but which are are not complex or time-consuming to create. A simple and effective notepad structure could be, for every communication, to record:

- the date (this can be defaulted to today's date so no keying is required)
- the type of communication (e.g. letter, telephone call, fax, meeting, that can be selected from a drop-down list)
- the direction of the communication (from the contact to you or from you to the contact)
- the subject of the communication (e.g. donation, pledge, complaint, sponsorship, etc., selected from a drop-down list)
- the result of the communication (e.g. pledge made, refusal, complaint, sponsorship, etc., selected from a drop-down list)
- one or more keywords that are searchable (selected from a drop-down list)
- some free-form notes.

This process takes a very small amount of time, creates an accurate history of your relationship with a contact/supporter and is an invaluable aid when making personal approaches in the future. When creating these notepad records you need fast access to the contact links/relationships feature because you will undoubtedly discover relationships, such as who knows whom, when discussing your cause with the contact. In fact, in some cases, the whole reason for your communication might be to find out who the person knows that they might approach for you. This brings up the subject of searching for contact records on the database.

Searching for contact records

Searching the database for a particular contact record may seem straightforward but it isn't. Mention was made on page 00 of keyed or indexed fields. You have to know what fields you are likely to search on and whether these fields are indexed or not. It is not acceptable, if Mrs Jones is on the telephone, for the system to take 30 seconds to find her record. (It does happen!)

Making a manageable enquiry

You will save yourself time if you know which fields in your database are actually searchable. Some systems allow you to search on contact number, surname, postcode, post town and little or nothing else. Similarly you should know which fields can be used in combination (e.g. it is useless to search a large UK database just for the surname 'Jones' because the likelihood is that you will find many hundreds of contacts that match your criteria. You need first initial or something else as well as surname in order to get a manageable list in response to your enquiry.).

You need to know which fields you really want to search on. Note that although it is technically possible to index every single field in the database, the more indexes you create the more overheads there are in the system and the less efficient it becomes – so be realistic.

Some typical search fields are:

- contact number
- postcode
- name (surname or organisation name)
- surname in conjunction with first initial
- first line of address
- post town
- telephone number
- e-mail address
- bank account number/ credit card number.

Essential facilities for searching include:

- searching with a combination of these fields
- searching with partial entries in any of the fields, e.g. postcode starts with 'RG'
- displaying a list of matching records in alphabetical order by name
- when displaying the list of matching records, being able to:
- highlight any record and click straight to the contact details and return to the list at any time with a single click
- display the contact details for the next record or the previous record in the list
- display the contact details for the first record or the last record in the list.

These are essential features. Some more sophisticated systems provide facilities like finding records by 'fuzzy matching' or 'sounds like matching', finding records by Keyword searches of Notepad areas and allowing you to define your own keyed fields – but don't bank on it!

Recording a diary of personal approaches

The next step from recording communications with people is to record future actions to be carried out by the contact, or by you, in relation to the contact. For example, you may wish to record a simple note dated one month from today, saying, 'Mr Jones suggested we call him today after he has received his share dividend.'

Two functions of the database system are vital at this point. One is to store the future actions in the same table (and display them on the same screen) as the communications discussed above, so that you can see the complete picture with relation to that contact. The other is to remind the user, on the due date, that an action is expected/required.

FIGURE 16 EXAMPLE OF A SIMPLE ACTION DIARY

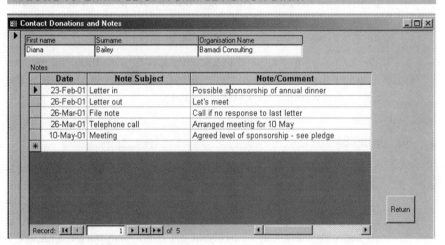

Other useful functions are:

- the ability to allocate/transfer actions to different users

- making a record of the status and result of the action in fields that can be searched (so that, for example, you could search for and print out all actions that are overdue and incomplete)

- automatic display of all incomplete actions at regular intervals

- the ability to postpone an action by changing the date

- the ability to filter actions so that you see either only your own actions or all actions against a contact, no matter who created them.

Recording and following up pledges . . .

Personal approaches might result in a pledge of money at a later date, rather than cash now or the promise of non-financial assistance of some sort. For example, 'I will speak to the minister next week when I see her' or 'I can't afford to give you anything now but I will speak to Mr Smith to see if he can help'. The system must have a facility to record and monitor the outcome of these pledges.

Data recorded about pledges will include:

- date of pledge
- amount of pledge and expected payment date
- a payment schedule for multi-payment pledges
- the campaign/appeal/segment code (or source code or approach code) if applicable
- the fund/project/sub-project (or earmark code) if applicable.

Functions related to this data include linking income received to the pledge and keeping a running balance, the production of regular monitoring reports and the ability to 'write-off' the outstanding balance of pledges that will not be fulfilled.

The information you need to keep track of for non-financial pledges is simply the date of the pledge, the action to be taken, the date of the action and whether it was taken or not.

. . . and legacies

Legacies are of fundamental importance to many voluntary organisations (some obtain more than 50 per cent of their total income from legacies). Everyone wants to increase the amount they get from legacies for many reasons, including the fact that a legacy is the single largest gift you are ever likely to get from a supporter. Chapter 7 describes the processes involved in managing the administration of legacies once obtained, but the process often begins with a personal approach to an individual to encourage them to make a bequest to your organisation.

The process will usually start with a selection and a mailing as described before. The database processes are as follows:

- identify and record people sent legacy marketing material (not just a specific and easily identifiable mailing history but a special legacy marketing indicator)

- record people who don't want legacy mailings and provide the facility to ensure that they don't get them

- record details of people who have made an enquiry about legacies

- record details of legacy pledges, including source of pledge, date and amount

- automatically exclude legacy pledgers from appeal mailings

- record details of visits to legacy pledgers

- record receipt of notification of legacy, status of legacy and amount received (this is the link with legacy administration).

Dealing with issues of ownership and security

The people who you approach personally are likely to be special and therefore require particular treatment, such as celebrities, high value donors or potential high value donors. You will normally have allocated a particular person in your organisation to make the approach and that person will cultivate a relationship with the contact/supporter. Consequently, you don't want other people approaching the same person, nor do you want distractions like general appeal mailings being sent to them. This brings up the dreaded subject of 'ownership' of contact records. Who in your organisation is responsible for the data and its accuracy? Who is authorised to modify the data? Who is allowed to produce mailings? Who is allowed to see the data? In short – who owns the data? In a small organisation this will not be a problem, but the larger an organisation becomes, the bigger this problem becomes.

The smaller and less expensive fundraising databases have no facilities in this area, but the larger and more expensive ones do.

Contact ownership functions in a database will include the following:

- Every contact is 'owned' by a single department or staff individual. This is recording the identity of the department or individual who entered the record to the database in the first place, who then becomes the 'owner' of the contact record and controls the access of other users to that record.

- Record against every contact, all other departments who 'have an interest in' the contact.

- Allow the 'owner' to transfer ownership to another department.

- 'Ownership' limits what details other departments can see of the contact, for example celebrity addresses, high value donor's giving history.

- 'Ownership' limits what groups of contact records a user can access, for example a volunteer can access individual donor records but not trusts or celebrities.

- 'Ownership' limits what functions other departments can carry out with respect to the contact, such as mailings or address changes.

Making approaches – events

Event management is an area where there are a large number of specialist packages available. However, if you run events, the people you want to invite to them will be on your main fundraising database, so ideally you want event management to be an integral part of that database. The sections below take you through how a database can assist you in planning and setting up the event in the first place, inviting people and dealing with their bookings, running the event itself, managing the financial aspects of the event and printing labels, lists and other reports.

Planning large-scale events

The first function will be to set up an Event record with basic details such as name, date, linked campaign code and fund code. This event record should be linked to a diary facility so that you can record future activities related to the event (e.g. 15 June – book venue, 30 July – pay deposit for venue). A venue file is also useful so that you can keep records of the various locations, facilities, capacities and costs. Once the event is created on the system you can start to add details like:

- a link to the venue file
- maximum delegate numbers
- budgeted income and expenditure
- seminars/sessions within the event (and their maximum numbers)
- equipment required generally and per session (with links to suppliers who might also be contacts on your database)
- helpers/organisers/stewards required
- speakers
- a schedule of delegate costs.

As the planning progresses and costs are incurred you need the facility to add actual costs to the event record that can be compared at any time with the budget. You should also be able to link sponsors to the event, both those who give money (and what it was for) and those who loan equipment or provide services.

Sending invitations and making bookings

Once the event is set up in the system you will usually invite people to attend. The people to be invited will be identified via one or more selections as described earlier. In addition to the functions described earlier under the heading of selections, there is another one for event management because the selected people need to be linked to the event as invitees. This applies even if people are invited on an ad-hoc personal basis because one form of selection described was 'manual' selection sets. The mailing generated after the selection is an invitation to the event in this case. In some instances the invitations will be general or will be included in large mailings that make it impractical to record everyone who was invited, in which case, this stage does not apply and invitees are not linked to the event.

Once people have been invited, whether directly or indirectly, you will start to receive bookings. There are many combinations to cater for. The easiest is the person who exists already on the database because a click to create a link to the event is all that is needed before adding details of the person's attendance details and requirements. These people are found by using the search functions described on page 30. The next easiest is the named person who is not on the database; in this case you add them as a new contact before linking them to the event and adding their attendance details and requirements. However, the system also has to cater for the known person who is bringing or booking for a number of un-named guests whose names we may never know, and also for secretaries/administrators from organisations who are booking for one or more of their colleagues whose names we may also never know.

Attendance details recorded per delegate may include type of delegate, cost, session preferences, special requirements such as wheelchair access or special diet, accommodation, travel arrangements, expected arrival time and other free-form notes. When recording event attendance data, the system must allow links back to other database functions, for example to record such things as address changes or to set up new membership records.

Managing large-scale events

The system must cater for:

- the creation and maintenance of waiting lists both for individual sessions and for the event as a whole
- cancellations and the refunding of money (with the subtraction of an administration fee if applicable)
- transfers between sessions within an event and transfers from one event to another
- multiple price lists (e.g. for different types of delegates)
- subsidies, discounts and free of charge places
- seat number allocation
- production of tickets (including multiple tickets for a single contact)
- multiple ticket types (e.g. two-day conference with two-day and one-day tickets)
- production of receipts/acknowledgements/confirmation letters
- documentation such as invoices, receipts and tickets being sent to someone other than the delegate
- allocation of helpers/stewards to their posts
- maintenance of equipment schedules
- production of meal schedules
- recording of who actually attended (as opposed to who booked to attend).

Managing the finances

When people book places at the event, the system should be able to produce invoices, including VAT accounting, as some element of the cost may be subject to VAT. Some database systems may handle this function through a batch link to an accounting system such as Sage. Payments for tickets (plus additional donations) must be accepted and recorded. The production of refunds or credit notes must be handled for cancellations. The system should also produce statements on request. The system should maintain running totals for income and expenditure and be capable of producing a simple profit and loss statement, but a link to a 'proper' accounting system is essential.

Reporting

The reports that can be produced by a database system are many and varied. They include the production of:

- badge labels
- attendee lists in a variety of sequences (e.g. by name, by organisation, or by session)
- individual session lists
- helper lists
- catering lists
- profit and loss statement
- non attenders list (booked but did not attend)
- payments due
- analysis of income by type of delegate
- comparative analysis of number invited versus number accepted/booked versus number attended.

Other fundraising events

So far we have looked at the database facilities associated with large-scale events such as conferences or annual dinners. Many fundraising systems do not provide all of these facilities and many charities do not need such comprehensive ones, especially if the only event of that type they organise during the year is their annual conference. Much more common is the need to manage fundraising events carried out by supporters.

Facilities required for managing smaller fundraising events are much more modest and well within the orbit of all fundraising databases. These facilities include the ability to:

- register the interest by a contact in organising a fundraising event
- record applications for the supporting material if you produce it (including a campaign/appeal/segment or source code and a fund/project/sub-project code if applicable – see Chapter 5)
- register the intention to hold an event and the date of the event
- record promotional items sent (e.g. balloons, posters)
- record income received from the event
- send a reminder letter if no money is received within three months of the event
- send a second reminder one month later.

These fundraising event facilities can be extended slightly to cover sponsorship events such as the London Marathon, a sponsored bicycle ride. The extension required might merely amount to: sending out a formal sponsorship form when the contact/supporter registers their intention to take part in a sponsored event; recording pledges if any are made before the event; or the creation of sponsored teams with a team leader, if applicable.

Distinguishing between event income and donations

Note that money raised in this way will normally be recorded on the database against the person organising the event or being sponsored because the names and addresses of the individual donors/sponsors is seldom known. In these cases the income has to be recognisable for what it is, event income as opposed to personal donations, and excluded from some of the analyses described in Chapter 5 on page 00, because to include it would give false results.

Making other types of approach

This section considers a number of other types of campaign approach. They are grouped together here because either they require a lesser level of database functionality than the approaches described in the previous sections of this chapter, or, as in the case of trading/mail order, they are seen to be of lesser importance by charities and other non-profit organisations in general.

The areas examined are community fundraising, raffles/lotteries and trading/mail order.

Community fundraising

Few fundraising databases contain specific functionality to assist community fundraising. So what is needed? In truth it is little more than coding people (usually volunteers) as particular types of contacts, recording income you receive from them (and designating it appropriately so that it does not skew the analysis in marketing reports such as RFV), and sending particular types of letters at various times. Consider the following types of approach.

Face-to-face

This is the person in the street who tries to sign other people up to committed giving schemes (standing orders or preferably direct debits). You need to code the person on the database as that type of fundraiser. (This will probably be an entry in one of your 'contact type' fields that can have several values because this person might also be a door-to-door collector and a volunteer who stuffs envelopes.) You then record the face-to-face fundraiser's own contact number against the standing order or direct debit when you set that up on the system. You can then run reports on the effectiveness of different face-to-face fundraisers. For example, who signed up whom and for how much, conversion rates (i.e. how many people actually started giving as opposed to the number that signed up) and drop-out rates over time.

Collection boxes

Code people as holders of collection boxes. You can then:

- run a selection from the database of all people to receive collecting boxes
- produce labels for boxes (box number, holder's name and database number)
- send letters (with tear-off response slip) and collecting box guidelines with boxes
- record to whom the boxes were sent (including recording the box numbers against the recipients), how many were sent, when they were sent and the expected return date
- record the return of boxes and the income received
- send reminder one month after box was due back if no cash has been received
- send second reminder one month later.

House-to-house collections

Code people as collectors. You can then:

- record details against collectors, such as local authority, street and house numbers to collect from, date range of their collection
- run a selection from the database of all collectors
- print collection labels
- send out collection envelopes to collectors
- record income received
- send thank-you letters
- send a reminder one month after the collection date if no cash has been received
- send a second reminder one month later

■ produce a report for a specified local authority on income and
expenditure related to the collections in their area.

Raffles and lotteries

The management of raffles or lotteries is a much neglected area of
almost all fundraising databases. Virtually none of the databases has
full facilities to manage raffles properly and yet almost all charities
run them, and can find themselves in theory operating illegally –
because if the Gaming Board were to ask, they would not be able to
match ticket numbers to the people to whom they have been sent!

In general terms, a Raffles system will maintain records of the raffle
itself, all raffle books sent to supporters/sellers, the serial numbers of
the tickets sent, the supporters/sellers they were sent to, the money
returned (ticket sales and donations) and the numbers of the ticket
stubs returned. More sophisticated features like re-order procedures
and the upgrading and downgrading of sellers so that they receive
more or less books next time can also be included. The system will
also reconcile ticket stubs returned with money returned, maintain
an audit trail and produce a series of financial, statistical and management reports.

At the time of writing, there were no fundraising databases that
incorporated a true lottery module, although there were a number of
standalone and bureau-based systems. A lottery system will maintain details of a weekly (or other frequency) draw, enter people into
the draw if they are 'paid-up', select a specified number of winners at
random upon request, and print reports such as a winners list, paid-
up players and non-paid-up players. More sophisticated facilities
include allocating players to collectors, printing 'payment due'
reminders and printing winners' cheques.

Trading and mail order

Almost every voluntary organisation sells things, even if it is only a
few Christmas cards, but very few fundraising databases have a
sophisticated trading/mail order/sales order processing module. This
probably reflects a lack of demand for it from the voluntary
organisations. Those who do very little in the way of product sales
record the money raised through the donation system as a special
type of income. Those who do a bit more by way of product sales
manage it in their accounts system. And those that do a lot by way of
product sales use specialist systems, of which a system called
Mailbrain is considered to be the best of breed. So what is it that the

few fundraising database mail order modules available do (or should do)? Facilities include:

- maintaining details of products and product groups
- processing sales orders
- automated calculation of delivery charges
- producing picking lists, delivery notes and invoices
- catering for cash with order and pro-forma invoicing
- catering for partial deliveries
- applying multiple price lists and multiple discount structures
- producing invoices
- full stock control including automated re-order levels, back order processing and stock write-offs
- processing order payments including donations and credit notes
- handling zero value items, sale or return items, alternative items (for items out of stock), returns and free of charge replacement
- producing refunds or credit notes as requested by customer for items out of stock
- bill of materials processing (or parts explosion) for at least one level (e.g. a pack of leaflets where each leaflet is also sold separately)
- maintaining details of suppliers, preferred suppliers, product delivery lead times and product costs on delivery for stock valuations
- reporting – sales summary by product and product group, sales summary by customer/contact type, best and worst sellers, stock valuation.

Handling customer care

Your donors/supporters/contacts are your customers. Without them you die as an organisation, so your database must be set up to enable you to look after them and give them what they want. This section of Chapter 6 describes the processes involved in thanking supporters for their support. This is the most important communication you will ever have with them. Also examined is the effective and efficient response to a customer's needs.

Thank-you letters

Most people want you to say 'thank you' when they send you some money, be it £5 or £5,000. The way you say it and how quickly you say it will leave a lasting impression on your donors. It is only polite, and certainly good policy, to make your thank-you letter as personal as possible, even if it is produced by an automated process.

The general rule is that the production of thank-you letters should be automatic after the entry of a batch of income items. Next, a few other requirements that the database system can help with:

- The donor requests that no acknowledgement is ever needed – code the donor's record accordingly so they never get a thank-you letter.
- The donor always requests an acknowledgement, no matter how small the donation may be – again, code their record.
- High value donors and celebrities need to be excluded from automated thank-you letter production – the system can remind you to write to them personally.
- Thank-you letters do not need to be sent for every standing order and direct debit payment, just for the initial setting up of the authority.
- Thank-you letters need to be produced in batches according to the 'owner' of the contacts, so they can be signed by the most appropriate person.
- Postage has to be minimised – thank-you letters and any requested information can be included in the same envelope.
- All letters can be viewed and amended if necessary before they are printed – many mistakes and wasted postage are avoided this way and letters can be personalised before printing where appropriate.

The actual production of the thank-you letters should be as flexible and as easy to set up as possible. Use Microsoft Word to create and maintain basic letter text if that is what you use for general word processing. Produce receipts instead of or as well as thank-you letters if requested (sometimes corporates and trusts want official receipts).

'Standard' thank-you letters can appear more personal if you:

- include different paragraphs according to system data, such as the campaign/appeal/segment code or the fund/project/sub-project code
- select different letters depending on contact type, for example individual or company or trust
- select different letters depending on income type, such as GAD (Gift Aid Declaration – see page 104) given or GAD not given
- include different paragraphs depending on the value of the donation
- include appropriate multiple paragraphs in a single letter for 'split' gifts

- include data items from the database into the letter text, such as the donation value.

  A few other things you could consider are:

- a response threshold so that any donation under a minimum amount never gets an acknowledgement

- text and letter cycling so that an individual never gets the same letter twice for multiple donations

- different digitised signatures according to the ownership of the contact from whom the donation came.

Giving donors what they want

Donors want to be thanked (well, most of them do!) They want you to get their name and address right. They want information and they want it quickly. They want to feel they are making a difference and not simply by contributing to core costs. They want to feel that you are using their money wisely and not wasting it. They don't want to be bombarded with mail every month.

If they ask you to send them something in the post they don't want you to telephone them. If they ask you to telephone them they don't want to receive some standard bumph in the post but no phone call. If they ask you to write to them only at Christmas then that is what they expect. If they say they don't want your product catalogue then you want to be sure that it has not been sent.

Your response

The key here is to be fast and accurate.

Don't let an information request get shunted around between departments where it might sit in an in-tray for days. An example here is tick boxes on donation forms one of which says 'Tick this box if you would like information on leaving us a legacy'. What often happens is that the donation information is entered and checked, the donation forms are filed, and those with ticked boxes are photocopied and sent to the appropriate department/person where they are dealt with as a second priority. Sometimes they even get sent to a mailing house to be fulfilled. Result – three, four or more weeks after the person ticked the box they get their information leaflet. Instead, when you first get the form, gather together the legacy information and get it ready to go with the thank-you letter or even get the system to produce a mailing label and send it out straightaway.

Don't allow cheques to sit around the office for days let alone weeks. Bank them on the day they arrive and get thank-you letters out to donors within three days of receiving the cheques at least. It can be done with good database systems, even in the largest of organisations. One simple control is to have the system produce a warning if no thank-you letter has been produced two days after entry of the income.

Keep the database clean. Check addresses regularly. Run the postcode checker (see pages 56–57) at least once a quarter to ensure you are up to date with postcode changes. You also need lots of mailing flags, category codes and interest codes (see pages 57–58). It is better to have too many than not enough. That way, with careful use of selection criteria, you can ensure that people get exactly what they want.

Complaints processing

All the processes required here have been described before, but it is worth reiterating them and bringing them together in one place because complaint handling is vital to the image of the organisation. All complaints must be logged on the database against the person making the complaint. Data that should be recorded includes:

- date of complaint
- type of complaint
- details/notes
- how notified
- who resolves
- how resolved
- lessons learned.

Actions taken must be recorded and complaint records should be visible along with all other information records, or it should be possible to filter information records and only view the complaint records (or any other single type of information record). A report listing all current complaints and their status should be produced at least once a week.

CHAPTER SEVEN

Monitoring

Having approached your supporters you need to be able to record their responses and to monitor how the campaign is going compared with the original plan. When recording responses, there is a huge number of different types of income to process, some with quite complex procedures, including Gift Aid, and a good database must be able to handle them all in the appropriate manner. Flexibility is the key to effective reports and the answer to this is a good industry standard report writing product such as Crystal Reports.

Income processing

Without the ability to enter details of all types of income you cannot create a fundraising database. Without access to all the procedures described below you cannot run an effective fundraising database. It may appear to be boring transaction processing but it is crucial not just for financial recording but for future fundraising campaigns (for example your Pareto and RFV analyses, see Chapter 5, are based on it). The section below covers:

- batching and banking processes
- the entry of the individual income items
- special processing for different types of income
- changes subsequent to the entry of transaction details and refunds
- some useful reports and analyses of income.

Batching and banking

Firstly, everyone needs to bank the money they receive, but is there a need for batch processing? Organisations that have very few income items per day, say less than 20, can find the relevant donors on the database and enter the details of the income items one at a time. But organisations that receive dozens, if not hundreds, of cheques per day need batching procedures for control and audit purposes.

What is a batch? A batch is a number of income items (usually between 20 and 50) grouped together with a control document (the batch header) that shows how many items are in the batch and their total value. This presupposes that you do some processing of the data before it enters the database (e.g. sorting and totalling). You may have sorted the incoming income into items of a similar type and made up batches of these similar items, grouping together all cheques for a particular campaign, for example, in which case this information will be included on the batch header as well.

The batch is created on the system and the control information (the number and total value of the items), is entered. At this stage you can also enter any other fields that are the same on all the items into the batch, for example the date, the campaign/appeal code, the fund code, the payment type, the payment method, and even the amount if they are all the same. Any such fields that you enter here will be defaulted in every income item so you won't have to enter them on every detail line. This saves a lot of data entry time. After you have entered the details of every income item in the batch, the system checks the totals against what you entered on the batch header as a control; you cannot finish the batch until the batch is 'reconciled', that is both the number of entries created and the total value matches the figures from the batch header.

Small and medium-sized organisations will usually enter all the details associated with each income item in one go as they progress through each batch. On the other hand, organisations with a very large number of income items per day often have a two-stage data entry process.

Stage 1 The first stage is the entry of 'skeleton' batches. This consists of creating the batch header and entering the amounts only of the income items. This is fast and means the money can be reconciled and banked quickly. The process is often carried out by finance staff who have little knowledge of the actual contacts/donors. At any point during the day you can request the system to produce a banking list for batches 'reconciled' so far. This will act as a control document for the money you take to the bank.

Stage 2 The second stage is 'completion' and is carried out by fundraising staff. It consists of the fundraiser calling up the batches on the system and entering the appropriate details: contact number, receipt yes/no, etc., against each amount. This will also involve some of the following income entry procedures.

Income entry procedures

Entering details of income items is not straightforward. There are many functions the system must perform during the entry of each item, for example:

- Link to an enquiry screen to search for a contact (because you will not always have a donation form with the donor's number neatly printed on it), select a donor and return to the income item with the selected donor's number inserted.

- Link to other functions (e.g. change of address or set up a membership record or enter a Gift Aid Declaration), and return to the income item.

- 'Split' a single item to different companies or different funds or even to different campaigns (e.g. a person specifies that their cheque covers their annual membership and a donation towards a particular project. The membership amount needs to be allocated to 'unrestricted funds' whereas the donation amount may need to be allocated to a particular restricted fund).

- Provide an automatic prompt when the contact/donor has an outstanding pledge, membership or other financial commitment and apply the item to it.

- 'Soft credit' another contact, for example Pauline Jones pays John Smith's membership so you put the actual income against Pauline Jones' record and a specially identified amount against John Smith's record so it appears that he has paid his membership. (The three important principles here are: the money is credited to the person who gave it, the person it was given for receives any benefits associated with its giving but it is not counted twice.)

- For an income item from an organisation, select the appropriate contact of the organisation to receive the thank-you letter from a list of named contacts (the named contacts list to include both those who are names only and those who are contacts in their own right – see page 62).

- Flag an item for further action (e.g. where a request is made for something, say a legacy leaflet, which needs to be sent with the thank-you letter).

- A useful, though not essential, feature is the ability to suspend the processing of a batch and call it up at a later time to finish it. This is helpful when there is a problem with an item that cannot be resolved immediately, so the operator can get on with other work, and when the operator goes for a break the batch is not left open on the screen.

Dealing with different types of income

The system must be able to process not just cash, cheques and postal orders but also other payment methods that have special procedures associated with them. These include:

- Credit cards (and CAF CharityCards) with the production of reports for the authorising bank/company, but preferably with a direct link to the bank/company for immediate payment authorisation.

- Vouchers (CAF and other) – most organisations treat these items like cash for accounting and reporting purposes but some treat them like a pledge and don't record them as actual income until after receipt of the report from the issuing agency and notification that the money is in the bank.

- Foreign currency – most organisations don't enter it into their database until the notice from the bank as to the sterling equivalent is received, others enter a dummy amount (often one penny) until the notice from the bank is received when the amount is changed; a very few systems have full foreign currency processing with exchange rates, exchange differences and confirming entries.

- Bank statements – there are often credits made directly to the bank that need to be entered to the database because they are donations; these are entered directly from bank statements. The main difference between these and other income items entered lies in the transfer of information to the accounting system.

For a discussion of the Bankers Automated Clearing System (BACS) procedure see page 102.

Post entry procedures

When a batch is both reconciled and completed, the items in it can be 'posted' to relevant contacts/donors and the details transferred, usually in a summary form, to the accounting system. However, there are things that may need to happen later that will alter the batch and its contents. These include the following procedures.

- Transaction amendment – this is usually for simple alterations: the fund code needs to be changed or the item was posted to the wrong supporter. Whatever the reason the system must have amendment procedures, usually only available to supervisors, so that the changes to the database and the appropriate accounting system adjustments can be made, allowing the database and the accounting system to be reconciled.

■ Reversals/refunds – there will occasionally be a need to reverse an entry completely (and make the appropriate ledger adjustment). In accounting terms there is a difference between a reversal (income never received, e.g. a bounced cheque) and a refund (income received but a refund cheque required) but most fundraising systems treat both the same, as a simple negative transaction, and leave the accountants to make manual adjustments!

Reporting and analysis

Once income has been entered to the database, any number of financial, statistical and management reports can be produced. Some that will be of immediate use for monitoring income received include:

■ a batch list showing every item in every batch for a specified day, and a summary for the day

■ a banking list showing every item in a specified banking on a specified day

■ a monthly banking summary

■ a daily income summary by payment method, e.g. cash, cheques, Visa, Access, CAF vouchers

■ a daily income summary by payment type, e.g. membership subscription, gift aided donation, non-gift aided donation, product sales

■ a daily credit card list by card type

■ a daily voucher list by voucher type

■ a daily transaction summary by campaign/appeal/segment code

■ a daily transaction summary by fund/project/sub-project code.

Keeping track of committed giving

Donations are great but unpredictable. Every organisation wants to get people signed up to some form of financial commitment that will help to even out their cash flow and ensure a long-term future for the organisation. Deeds of covenant (though still valid) are effectively gone, so other forms of committed giving are increasingly important. This section of Chapter 7 looks at:

■ membership and subscription schemes and their administration

■ the management and processing of standing orders and direct debits

- payroll giving
- corporate matched giving.

Membership and subscriptions

Many organisations talk about their 'members', but they are not members in the formal sense of belonging for a period of time on payment of an annual fee. What follows is a description of a full membership system. Note that if you do not run a membership scheme like this then don't talk to database suppliers about 'membership' because it is always a separate module at additional, and sometimes quite large, cost.

The first specific data table required is a member table containing things like type of member (individual, family, unwaged, corporate, etc.), status (provisional, active, lapsed, etc.), annual fees, joining date, renewal date, branch affiliation. You also require a grade and rates table before you can get started.

Membership system functions include:

- allowing one contact to have more than one membership
- handling free of charge and lifetime memberships (i.e. they do not receive renewal notices)
- coping with non-standard time periods (e.g. initial period of 15 months followed by 12 monthly renewals)
- gift membership (actual payment against the giver and soft credit against the member)
- maintaining a list of publications to which the member is entitled by member type
- recording incentives sent to member/prospective member
- entering receipt of membership fees and additional donations
- printing invoices and/or receipts as required
- printing membership cards
- an automated process for creating and printing renewals and reminders with the ability to check and amend them before printing
- automatic 'lapsing' after the third reminder when the status will be set to lapsed and no more publications will be sent
- printing and distributing ballot papers
- producing mailing labels for publications
- printing member statistics (e.g. numbers by sex, geographic region, status, type, campaign code, fund code, movements over time)

- printing branch directory (by the 3-tier regional structure, listing all the post-holders)
- printing branch list (i.e. a list of all changes to membership since the last time it was printed: new, lapsed, deceased, etc.)
- printing list of current members, lapsed members, deceased members, new members.

Subscriptions are remarkably similar to memberships in database system terms and are often handled in the same module. A contact can have one or more subscription records, each of which defines a publication they receive, the number of copies they receive, the frequency of publication, the cost and the renewal date. The same functions as for membership will apply except there will be no printing of membership cards or ballot papers (two things that many organisations don't do anyway in their membership schemes).

Regular giving – standing orders

When a supporter signs a standing order, the bank automatically sends the receiving organisation the money every month (or other specified period) until the supporter cancels the order. So the first thing you need to do with the database is to create a standing order record for the supporter that details their:

- bank sort code
- bank account number
- bank account name
- the regular amount expected
- the date the first payment is due
- the frequency of the payments so that you can check them when they arrive.

For some small organisations, the only indication that the money has been received is when the entries appear on the bank statement. Most banks now supply files of standing order payments that you can load directly into your system. These files sometimes come on disk or via a telephone connection with the bank but increasingly they can now be received via an e-mail attachment.

If you get a file from the bank, your database system must be able to:

- read it
- create income batches for control purposes in the same way as you create them manually (except that it might just create one great big batch for the whole file)

- match the payments with the correct supporters
- hold in a suspense account and report on items it cannot match to a database contact

Your system should be also be capable of producing a series of control reports such as: a full list of items received; unmatched items;payments received but not expected (i.e. it matched a payment to a supporter but no payment was due according to the schedule); payments expected but not received (i.e. a list of the supporters with standing orders whose due payment date was before the date of the file but no payment was received from them). There must then be a process for the user to examine the unmatched items and post them to supporters as they are identified. As a last resort these will be posted to the anonymous donor record.

Regular giving – direct debits

The committed giving method that most organisations are trying to encourage their supporters to adopt is direct debit because you can control when the money comes in and you can increase the amount as and when you wish (as long as you inform the donor of course!). This is particularly useful for memberships, subscriptions and various sponsorship schemes as you do not have to rely on the donor contacting their bank to upgrade a standing order. The first thing you need to do with the database is to create a direct debit record for the supporter that details their:

- bank sort code
- bank account number
- bank account name
- the regular amount to be received
- the start date
- the finish date
- the frequency of the payments.

Bankers Automated Clearance Service (BACS)

The system will have a facility for you to create a file to transmit to the bank using BACS, the Bankers Automated Clearing Service, at regular intervals. The system will look through the direct debit records and create a claim for any payments that are due, the file will be created, the income items added to the supporter records and the file sent to BACS. A control report detailing the payments requested from BACS will be printed.

Credit card payments

Some people pay memberships and subscriptions by credit card. Credit card revolving authorities operate in almost exactly the same way as direct debits. You create a file of transactions to be claimed in the same way as direct debits. The major difference with these authorities is that all credit cards have an expiry date and you have to keep going back to the supporter to get the authority renewed.

Payroll giving

This is the scheme through which employed people give money to charity by having it deducted directly from their salary. The money is collected from the participating employers by an agency (the Charities Aid Foundation scheme GAYE – Give As You Earn – is the biggest one) who then pass it on to the relevant charities (less their commission). Similarly to the banks and their standing order files, CAF and some of the other agencies supply details of the payments on a file that can be loaded directly into the database. The other relevant factor here is that some charities use professional recruitment agents to sign up payroll givers for a fixed fee per giver signed up.

Database functions required are to:

- link the giver to their employer
- link the giver to the recruiter (if applicable)
- produce thank-you letters when people enter the scheme
- link the employer to the agency that collects the money
- import payment details directly from the file if the agency provides one (matching on the agency's own unique reference number for the giver) or enter them manually from listings if not.

Your system should also be capable of producing a series of management reports such as: total income received; received not expected; expected not received; and promised not yet started.

A further level of sophistication can be added by creating a payroll-giving record for every giver, recording the recruitment cost, keeping a running total of payroll giving donations and hence being able to report on the profitability of individual payroll givers, payroll givers associated with particular recruiters and payroll givers as a whole.

Corporate matched giving

This scheme involves an employer agreeing to match any amount raised for a particular charity by their staff. You can, if you wish, create a link from the employee/s to the employer, create a pledge for the employer when income is received from employees, print comparison reports of employee/employer payments and send a payment reminder list to the employer. Quite frankly this is best handled outside the system in a personal manner because it is a large administrative overhead for little benefit. Just record any income received from employees and employers as normal but with a suitable income type to indicate that it was matched giving.

Other special procedures

This section of Chapter 7 discusses a collection of important administrative areas that require special procedures.

Gift Aid

This is so important to every charity that the database must handle it and handle it well. The first thing to get right is the recording of the donor's GAD (Gift Aid Declaration). Most charities are encouraging their supporters to sign a global declaration that covers every donation they have made since the scheme started and every donation they will ever give in the future, so many are simply recording 'GAD given = Yes' and the date it was given. But, donors, if they want it, have complete flexibility over their declarations. You really need to record:

- taxpayer = Yes/No
- GAD given = Yes/No
- how given
- date given
- date withdrawn
- valid from date
- valid until date
- confirmation letter sent = Yes/No
- date sent for oral declarations
- and even a 'GAD refused = Yes/No' field so that you know if they have been asked before and said 'No'.

Once you have all this sorted out you can consider the functions of the database.

Every gift received from an individual must be checked to see if you have a valid GAD that covers it. If you have, then fine. If you haven't, but the person has refused to sign a GAD, then that is the end of the matter. If you haven't, and the person hasn't refused to sign before, then you have to decide if you are going to ask them again (because you have probably asked more than once already). At regular intervals you will ask the system to produce a tax claim for all donations from individuals for whom you hold a valid GAD and for which you haven't claimed tax before. It is helpful if this report can be run without updating the database so that you can review it before you actually make the claim from the Revenue. When you run this report for real, the system will mark the donations it has claimed for and print the claim in a format acceptable to the Revenue.

When the cheque for your claim is received from the Revenue then you have two options for dealing with it.

1 Record the Revenue cheque against a donor called Inland Revenue (or don't record it in the database at all, just in the accounting system – in which case, to see the real value of your donors you will need a 'grossing up' report or view on the screen that shows the actual donations received, and also a gross figure calculated by the system for donations covered by a GAD).

2 The system stores a copy of every detailed tax claim it makes and when an Inland Revenue cheque is received you select the appropriate claim and run a process that 'splits' the cheque to the individual donors according to the claim. In this case you then get two actual figures against every donor – one for the actual donation and one for the tax received from the Revenue in respect of the donation.

In addition, you need a reversal procedure for the unlikely event that a claim is rejected by the Revenue and you need some financial, statistical and management reports such as potential Gift Aid donations this day, week or month showing net and gross, overdue GAD letters, new GADs this day, week or month, and GADs refused.

Legacy administration

A rule of thumb expressed by some people is that if you receive more than about 30 legacies per year you should consider a legacy administration system. There are specialist systems for this process that do just this, one is called First Class (and lives up to its name by all accounts) and another is Lawbase Legacy Administration. A small number of the fundraising databases do have a legacy administration module. What functions do they/should they provide? Apart from the particular items of data that need to be recorded, all of the required functions have been described before. It is just a case of bringing them together for the legacies administrator.

On notification that your organisation has been mentioned in a will, you will create a legacy record and link it to a contact (who may or may not be on your database already). Important data items in this record are:

- date of will
- date of death
- type of legacy (residuary, pecuniary, specific, discretionary)
- value of bequest
- percentage of estate total
- type of bequest (cash, shares, property, etc.)
- links to executors, solicitors, next-of-kin and any other charities that are sharing in the will.

The most important thing now is a good diary function so that you can record when things are supposed to happen and you can see a history of things that have happened (or were supposed to happen). You now need:

- a link to word processing for writing letters to all the parties involved
- to be able to record payments received (and any expenses you incur)
- to be able to make and record tax claims and produce a wide range of reports.

Some useful reports which your system should produce are: income to-date from open cases; future income expected (and when); income breakdown by legacy type; income breakdown by contact type (male/female, member/non-member, etc.)

More sophisticated systems might provide:

- last and previous addresses (recognising that a person's last address is often a nursing home and not necessarily where they lived when they made their will) for demographic analysis for future legacy marketing
- scanning, storage and retrieval of all legal documents and correspondence associated with the case.

In memoriam processing

People frequently give donations in memory of a deceased person, often in place of buying flowers for the funeral. This is another area where you can make good use of the concept of soft credits (see page 97).

Firstly, you have to make the decision as to whether you process money you receive against the deceased or against the person or organisation (often it comes via the funeral director) that gave it. This is an important decision because you will need to produce a report on income received in memory of a person for their relatives. The way many people achieve this is to process the money against the deceased and a soft credit against the actual donor. The donor and any dedication can be recorded in a 'notes' field of the income item. It is now easy to produce a list of all donations given in memory of a particular person because they are all recorded against that person with all the necessary information. Equally, it can be done the other way around with the donations recorded against the actual donor and a soft credit against the deceased.

Recording corporate sponsorship

Companies will often sponsor core costs as opposed to (and hopefully in addition to) giving straight donations. You need a mechanism for identifying and recording this type of support. This is provided by pledges as described in Chapter 6, page 82. For straight financial support you record an income pledge, such as what the company is paying for (costs of the annual review, costs of a project, etc.), the pledged amount and when it will be paid. You then record the income when received as per normal but link it to the pledge. Note that when viewing the income associated with any campaign on the one hand or any fund on the other hand, it is useful to be able to separate out corporate sponsorship from donated income.

For indirect financial support you record a non-income pledge or an information record, for example the company provides the venue for an event, so no money changes hands but it has a value to you in terms of an expense that you didn't incur, or the company pays for the printing of the annual report, etc. In such cases you assign a 'notional' value to the item.

Consolidation and analysis

Sophisticated computer systems are no good at all unless you can analyse the data and extract it in the format you want it. How many times have you heard someone say, or even said it yourself, 'It's in there somewhere but I can't get it out!'? A fundraising database will have a large number of standard reports that should give you all the analysis you need on a day-to-day basis. It should also provide you with tools to produce your own special reports and tools to take extracts of data out of the system completely in order to put it into other systems for further manipulation and analysis.

Standard reports produced by fundraising databases

So what should you expect from your system? Some systems come with a basic set of 20 pre-programmed reports and others come with over 200 pre-programmed reports. Here are a few that you will find absolutely essential:

- daily detailed batch list
- banking list
- income summary by day, week, month and year-to-date
- income summary by campaign/appeal/segment
- campaign/appeal/segment analysis and ROI (Return On Investment)
- income summary by fund/project/sub-project
- income summary by payment method
- income summary by payment type
- potential Gift Aid income for day, week, month and year-to-date
- standing order & direct debit expected not received
- standing order & direct debit received not expected
- high value donor report
- pledge status report
- cash flow report
- various counts of donors by type and category, such as GAD versus non GAD, direct debit versus non direct debit
- standing order or direct debit drop-out rates
- members by type
- members by status
- subscriptions list
- Pareto analysis
- Recency/Frequency/Value analysis
- full contact details (for Data Protection Act purposes – see Chapter 10).

Report writers

All but the simplest systems provide you with the ability to produce your own reports. Some have their own bespoke report generator but there is a growing trend towards simply integrating an industry standard report generating system into the package. After all, you buy a packaged database in order to avoid re-inventing the wheel, so the fundraising database suppliers do it too. The most common report generating system is Crystal Reports. This is almost a de facto industry standard reporting system today, particularly as it is capable of reading files or tables from all of the major database development systems: Access, SQL Server, Oracle, FoxPro, dBaseIV, etc. Many of the fundraising databases use Crystal Reports as their report writer and the best of them provide their own standard reports written in Crystal, so if you find a standard report that is *almost* what you want, then you can modify it in a couple of minutes and have the report *exactly* how you want it.

A big word of warning is required here. Writing your own reports from a fundraising database is not as easy as it sounds. You may have an easy to use report writing system but you still have to understand the structure of the files in the database in order to create reports that make sense. This is easy if all you have is a contacts table, a gifts table and an appeals table, but what happens when your database has 600 linked tables and the data you want to report on is contained in 10 of them? The concept of 'wizards' help to overcome this inevitable gap between fundraising and the technology, but it is still no mean task to create the report and get it right. You may need a database expert to help you out. Of course, you may have no choice but to produce your own reports if you possess one of the flexible database systems and you have added lots of your own data fields.

Links with other systems

In some cases you might just want a simple analysis that you would normally do in Excel or Access and cut and paste into management reports. In this case the database must be able to output the data you require in a suitable format so that you can use such systems if you wish. Most databases have a relatively simple export feature so that you can do this. Similarly if you just can't get the level of analysis you want out of the database (maybe you want to use a statistical package such as SPSS for calculating an analysis of variance, linear regression, etc.) then the system must export data, in detail or summary, as requested, and in an appropriate format for direct input to SPSS or other packages. There is nothing worse for a user than having to waste time manipulating tables and formats in order to import data into another system.

The other major system link employed by many organisations is with their accounting system. For small charities this is a waste of time. If all your accountant needs in the Nominal Ledger is one entry per month for each income type then this is best entered by hand as a single journal at the end of the month from information provided by the fundraising system on a month end income summary report. If, on the other hand, your organisation has hundreds of income items per day, then an automatic (or semi-automatic) link between the fundraising database and the Nominal Ledger is essential. A very few systems provide a direct link such that as you enter a transaction into the database then it automatically goes into the Nominal Ledger at the same time. However, this is not the norm and, in fact, most accountants don't like it because they don't have control over what is entered to their ledgers. The normal method of operation is for the database to produce a CSV (or ASCII) file that the accountant can import into the ledger at their leisure. In rare instances this file consists of every single income item, if that is the accountant's request. But, usually, the database will summarise the income items according to rules that you specify. These rules are such things as one transaction per campaign/appeal code per batch per day. In this way there is far more control over the processing. The two systems are kept in step with each other in a controlled and easily reconcilable manner.

CHAPTER EIGHT

Database administration

A database, of any type, does not manage itself. It needs help. Do not think, as some people do, that all your worries are over the moment you buy a fancy new database, that the money will roll in and the database will look after itself. It won't happen unless you make it happen. Firstly, you need a system supervisor or database administrator, or preferably two so that you have cover for holidays and sickness. This chapter looks at the responsibilities of this administrator, who controls access to the system, maintains its integrity, builds the new screens if that is part of the system, carries out routine tasks, carries out complex tasks for users, trains new staff in its operation, provides a first line of support and generally becomes the fount of all knowledge with respect to the database. If you don't have a database administrator then your system will gradually fall into disuse.

Supervisor functions

Every system needs a supervisor. There will be new users to add to the system. This might be a simple process of typing in a name (often called the 'user ID') and a password, but it is more than likely that it will involve creating a whole 'user profile'. This means adding a new user name and password and also defining exactly which screens the person can view, which processes the user can run, which contacts the user can view and which contact records the user can modify. There will be old users to remove when people leave the organisation. There will be passwords to set up (and change when people forget them). There will be tables to manage in order to maintain consistency; remember the N Yorks, North Yorks and North Yorkshire difficulty on page 56? There will be regular processes to run and check for correct operation, such as direct debit file creation or looking for and merging duplicate records. There will be regular reports to run, such as Gift Aid tax claims. There will be general and/or potentially dangerous processes to run, such as global updates. (Global updates need great care because a small mistake can alter the contents of a database permanently with no means of recovery. More on global updates later in this chapter.) There may even be backups of the database to take, but hopefully that will be taken care of by the overall system backup procedures.

Audit, security and control

The database system itself must contain features to ensure effective, efficient, accurate, consistent and complete operations.

Audit

The system must provide an audit trail. There are two aspects to this that you should consider. The first is being able to identify an income item when (and where) it arrives in the organisation and follow its progress through the system, for example from the batch it was included within, via the contact to whom it was allocated, to the Nominal Ledger journal it was included within. The second is being able to identify who entered what transactions to the database or who made what changes to contact records, and when. This entails having a user ID and a date and time on every record. Some systems allow two IDs, dates and times; one for when the record was first created and one for the last time it was modified. This is particularly useful to track changes, for example when an address is changed and someone else changes it back again.

Security

Security features such as user IDs and passwords have been mentioned above. They are absolutely essential to prevent misuse of the system and, more importantly, misuse of the data within the system. After all, the data in the system is your most important asset, so you must look after it. Stories abound in the industry concerning the misuse of data, including the one about the volunteer who printed off a list of high value donors and then wrote to them privately.

Access to various functions should be controlled by passwords and the system should force users to change their passwords at regular intervals. Every system comes configured with a 'default' user ID and password and it is amazing how many organisations you can walk into, who may have been using their database for years, type in the supplier default and get into every function of the system!

The system should allow the following restrictions depending on a combination of user ID and password:

- restrict access to specific modules/menus/functions

- restrict access to specific screen displays

- restrict access to specific reports

- restrict access to specific selections

- restrict access to specific sets of contact records (e.g. only the Trusts department can see trust records)

- restrict access to specific parts of contact records (e.g. protecting celebrity addresses or restricting who can see bank account details)

- restrict access to specific types of operation (e.g. who can view, who can input and who can update).

Control

The system must contain features to ensure that every operation it starts is completed and not stopped halfway through, or if it does stop halfway through for some reason, the system informs the user and provides an audit trail so that the user knows where it has got to. Typical areas where this is critical is the allocation of batched income items to the individual contacts, the processing of a bank standing order or a CAF file, the transfer of summary data to the accounting system, the output of a selection for a mailing house, etc.

The database should also have internal processes to ensure that the data within it remains consistent. This is known as maintaining the database integrity. A prime example is not allowing contacts to be deleted if there are income items still attached to them (or if you really want to delete the contact, then deleting all the associated records as well). In addition, there should be the facility to recover to a consistent position if the database does crash (and it does happen) for any reason. A crash could have an external cause, such as someone turning the power off whilst the database was performing some processing, or there could be a system error. Whatever the cause, if the database is not closed down properly, then when it is restarted, it should check itself for consistency and if an inconsistency is found then either inform the user of the problem, or, as in the case of large database systems, 'roll back' to the last consistent state (and tell the user what it has done).

Data management

The supervisor will have many regular tasks to perform to keep the data 'clean' and up-to-date. Adding entries to system tables is one of these tasks. These tables include the master lists of:

- contact types
- income types
- payment methods
- campaign codes
- fund codes, etc.

Adding entries to these tables needs to be a supervisor function so that the tables and the coding structures remain consistent and existing reports continue to be effective. For example, consider the introduction of a new fundraising campaign. It might be called the Summer 2001 Campaign but if a new campaign code was added to the Campaigns Table as 'Summer 2001' when all the previous campaigns were defined with the year first, '2001 Spring' and so on, then the reports produced will not be in a consistent sequence.

Dealing with duplicate records

Identification of and dealing with duplicate records is another important task.

The database system should have a standard process for searching the entire database for possible duplicates according to criteria the user has specified (e.g. surname and postcode). When it has identified possible duplicates it must provide the user with options for every pair, or more, of possible duplicate records that it finds. The first is to ignore them if they are in fact different contacts. The second is to merge them together if they are the same contact. In this case the user has to specify which record is to stay and which record is to be merged/deleted. This merging is an extremely complex process as it entails identifying all the records in any table that are linked to the contact to be removed, unlink them, relink them to the contact that is staying and delete the other contact record. The smaller and less sophisticated databases cannot carry out this process and you have to do it by hand by deleting records and typing them in again.

Global updating

Global updating of data is another important supervisor function. If you use postcode software, then every three months there will be a process to put in the new PAF and change the postcodes on existing contact records where the Royal Mail have re-coded their addresses. This is a very simple routine task. Of more interest is a generalised global updating function within the database. This is where you specify a set of criteria to search for contacts and then specify a set of changes to be made to the records of those contacts. A prime example is the change of telephone number prefixes. Another example is to set a 'Special donor' flag on anyone who has given more than £1,000 in the last 12 months. This is a glorified 'search and replace' function, but it is so powerful and potentially so dangerous (you can easily corrupt your entire database), that it must be done under strict control.

Import and export

Every database will have an import routine, if only to add new names and addresses from an external data file. The data has to be mapped from the source, usually an Excel spreadsheet or a text file, onto the appropriate fields in the database. A good database will allow you to import data into ANY field in the entire database, but essential imports are names and addresses and income items. Income items might come to you on files from the bank (standing orders), CAF (payroll giving) or even a fulfilment house if you had a very large campaign and had your income processed by a third party. The database should accept a variety of data formats so that the process is as easy as possible. With regard to data import, there might be the added complication of reciprocal data files received from other organisations to deal with. All these imports need to be defined, tested, carried out and checked. This is definitely a supervisor function.

Conversely, there will be times when you want to export data from the database. Names and addresses for mailing houses, names and addresses for demographic profiling (and then importing the results), names and addresses for reciprocal mailings, direct debit details for the bank and the transfer of income summary information to the accounting system are the main ones you will come across regularly. In a similar way to imports, these exports need to be defined, tested, carried out and checked. Again this is a supervisor function.

Complex selections and reporting

Fundraisers must know quite a lot about their database, how it is built and how it works in order to use it effectively. But they are not, and should not be, computer system experts, so learning how 600 tables link together is unlikely to be high on their personal agenda. However, someone in the organisation needs to know how this works if you want to do very complex analysis, segmentation, selection and reporting. The more you use the database, the more sophisticated things you will want to do with it, which is where a database administrator with a deeper knowledge of the system is essential. Fundraisers can then run simple queries, reports and selections and 'ask the expert' to do it when the task becomes complex.

CHAPTER NINE

Beyond fundraising

There are other facilities that are sometimes found in contact databases that are only indirectly related to fundraising. They are, however, definitely related to contacts. The first is requests by you for information from your contacts in the form of questionnaires. The rest are related to where the money goes rather than where it comes from and are associated with the much neglected, by computer systems, care or operational side of your organisation. Areas covered are project sponsorship, beneficiary systems (grant giving as opposed to grant getting), research grant management and Helpline support.

Questionnaires and information requests

You are, or should be, continually asking your supporters for information about themselves. The more you know, the better you can target your appeals and the more effective your fundraising will be. Some databases allow you to define additional data tables (including editing rules and drop-down lists) and screens (or forms) to enter data into these tables. Consequently, you can design a questionnaire, duplicate its appearance on a screen in the database, create a table to hold the responses and enter individual contact's answers to the questions. When every respondent's answers have been entered, you can then analyse the responses using the database system's report writer.

This applies only if you want to know and use relevant things about individuals, such as their age, number of children, projects they are interested in. If you simply want to gather statistics such as what percentage of your supporter base is vegetarian, then you would use a spreadsheet.

FIGURE 17 EXAMPLE OF A SIMPLE QUESTIONNAIRE ENTRY FORM

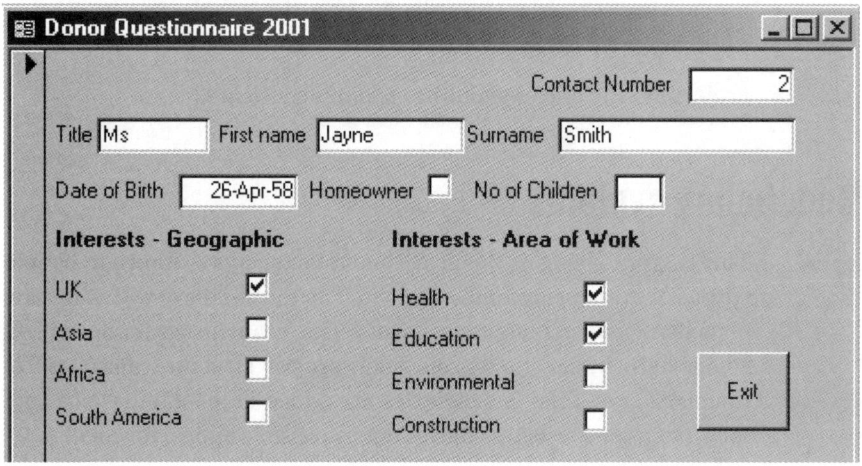

Project sponsorship

Many charities run 'sponsorship' schemes where supporters are asked to provide financial assistance for an individual project. Project is used in the loosest sense here because supporters could be sponsoring a well for fresh water in Africa or a child's education or a granny or a donkey or a swan or whatever other area or beneficiary group you work with. The reason that some fundraising systems have these facilities is the direct link between the project/beneficiary and the donor/supporter/contact. So projects are created on the database and one or more sponsors are linked to the project. One supporter can sponsor many projects and one project can have many sponsors.

The project will have a start date, an end date, budgeted costs, and a minimum sponsorship level per annum. Sponsors commit a minimum amount for a minimum period of time and the money is usually collected by standing order or direct debit. As the money arrives a running total is maintained for the project and compared against the budgeted costs for the project. As sponsors drop out of the scheme, new ones are recruited and as one project comes to an end the sponsor is offered a new one. Sometimes the database system contains the concept of recording pledges for support of a project that will not start until the target has been reached, such as building a new wing for a hospice.

Some of the reports out of the system are:

- list of all projects with their sponsors

- pledges to-date versus target
- projects over or under subscribed
- income to-date versus target
- project income and expenditure by financial years.

Beneficiary systems

This is grant giving or the provision of financial assistance to beneficiaries. A grant programme is created on the database with aims and objectives and a budget to spend. The grant programme will fit somewhere in the fund/project/sub-project structure discussed in Chapter 4. Potential beneficiaries are added to the database as contacts (identified as beneficiaries not as possible appeal targets!).

- Requests for information/application forms from potential beneficiaries are logged.
- Formal grant requests/applications are logged and acknowledged.
- A diary facility is required for follow-up actions regarding the applications.
- An application status is maintained.
- Applications are marked as accepted or rejected.
- A payment schedule for the beneficiary is defined (e.g. £20 per month for 4 years)
- Any criteria to be met before payments are made are defined.
- A regular process creates payments, usually as a file of transactions or a listing that is input to the accounting system Purchase Ledger for cheques to be printed or BACS payments made.

Reports that your database system should produce include: application requests made; applications received; grants approved/rejected; payments made this week, month or year; funds remaining in each programme; full programme financial status, including budgeted payments versus actual payments versus payments yet to be made.

Research grants

The management of research grants is very similar to the process for individual grants above, except that there is usually a complex approval process involving references and committees (more contacts to be linked and more status indicators on the application) and every single payment has to be authorised.

Helplines

Full Helpline systems are very complex and specialist packages are available in this area. However, some simple systems exist in a few of the contact databases that deal with the major requirements of Helplines for charity beneficiaries. The beneficiaries are entered onto the database. When a call comes in a helpline record is created and linked to the beneficiary. This record contains details such as:

- enquiry source
- duration of call
- subject area
- outcome/further actions required
- keywords (for searching purposes, e.g. who on the database has had a similar problem?)
- unlimited notes.

The callers may be given information/advice that is recorded on their Helpline record and may be given the contact details of someone who can help them, for example a doctor, other health professional, volunteer helper. In this case the caller's contact record is linked to the record of the doctor/helper, etc., via the relationships function.

In some cases the caller's record details are retrieved and the helpline record is created as the caller is on the line. In other cases, especially for sensitive medical situations, written notes are taken at the time of the call and the helpline records are created at a later time.

CHAPTER TEN

The Data Protection Act

Your database contains 'personal data' and this therefore obliges you by law to comply with the Data Protection Act. This chapter describes the eight parts of the Act, defines 'personal data' and explains the distinction between personal data and 'sensitive' personal data. It discusses your legal responsibilities, and the rights of the people whose information you hold, under the Act. It also introduces the Telecommunications Regulations 1999 (Data Protection and Privacy), as these are relevant to charities fundraising or promoting their cause by phone or fax.

When you hold personal data, you must be aware of the following points:

1 The information you hold on people (known as data subjects) and the use you make of it has to adhere to eight principles – these principles cover things like fairness, compliance with the law, relevance, accuracy, the length of time you keep data, rights of data subjects, loss or damage, and transferring data outside of Europe.

2 A data subject can request a copy of the data you hold about him/her, the reasons you are holding it, and have the data corrected or erased where appropriate.

3 You have to 'register' with the Information Commissioner – this is known as Notification.

The latest data protection legislation is the 1998 Data Protection Act and it came into force on 1 March 2000. It affects every fundraising organisation. If you think you are exempt, then you are wrong. *And even more than this, you have to comply with the provisions of the Act even if you don't register.*

The theory

There are eight parts or 'Principles' to the Data Protection Act 1998. These are as follows.

1 **Personal data must be processed fairly and lawfully**
You must tell data subjects (people on whom you hold data) what you will do with the data or the processing has to be necessary (e.g. for legal or medical reasons).

2 **Personal data is obtained only for specified and lawful purposes**
You should tell both the data subjects and the Information Commissioner what these specified purposes are. (The Information Commissioner was previously called the Data Protection Commissioner, and before that the Data Protection Registrar. The change to the current name reflects the fact that the Commissioner now administers the Freedom of Information Act as well as the Data Protection Act.)

3 **Personal data shall be adequate, relevant and not excessive**
Beware of recording things about people 'because it might be useful in the future' – this contravenes the Act. For example, both daytime and evening telephone numbers – Do you need both? Will you have any need for both?

4 **Personal data shall be accurate and up to date**
Regular data cleaning is essential. Beware of default settings – they might not be accurate. You have to make reasonable efforts to ensure the accuracy of the data.

5 **Data shall not be kept for longer than is necessary**
There is an ongoing debate in fundraising about deleting contact records. Should you ever delete supporter records, for example people from whom you haven't heard for 10 years? They might give a legacy and you would want to know if they were previously a supporter or not.

6 **Data shall be processed in accordance with the rights of the data subjects**
The rights of data subjects are:

– The right of subject access; in order for people to find out what information you hold about them.

– The right of rectification, blocking, erasure and destruction; people can apply to the Court to have data rectified, blocked, erased or destroyed if it is inaccurate or contains opinions which are based on inaccurate data.

– The right to prevent processing; if that processing could cause damage or distress.

- The right to prevent processing for purposes of direct marketing; this is an absolute right so you need to be careful about the exact nature of the things that you send to your supporters.

- The right to compensation; people can claim compensation from you for damage and distress caused by a breach of the Act.

- Rights in relation to automated decision-taking (including the right to have logic explained): people can insist that no decision which *significantly affects them* is based on processing data in any automatic manner.

You have 40 days to comply with a request from an individual to see the data you hold about them and you can levy a small fee (up to £10), but your database must be able to produce a complete record of everything you hold on an individual upon request.

7 **Appropriate technical and organisational measures shall be taken to prevent unlawful processing and loss of or damage to the data**
Beware of hackers, it is your responsibility to keep them out. Beware of getting rid of old computers – reformat the disk first.

8 **Personal data shall not be transferred outside the European Economic Area unless that country provides an adequate level of protection**
There are problems with America and lots of other countries who do not have equivalent data protection legislation, but 'get outs' include when the data subject gives consent to the transfer or the transfer is in the interests of the data subject.

What is personal data?

Personal data is any information about living, identifiable individuals. This includes their name and address, telephone number, any classification codes you assign to them, any other flags assigned to them, such as 'do not mail' indicators, interest indicators, also any notes you keep about them *and* a donor's full giving history. You can hold this data without the individual's specific sanction (as long as you comply with all the elements of principle 6).

However, there is a distinction drawn between personal data and 'sensitive' personal data. Sensitive personal data is anything to do with:

- racial or ethnic origin
- political opinion
- religious or other beliefs
- trade union membership

- physical or mental health or condition
- sexual life
- commission or alleged commission of any offence
- any proceeding for an offence or alleged commission of an offence, the disposal of or sentencing in such proceedings.

The main reason for the distinction is that 'explicit' consent from the data subject is required before you can hold and use 'sensitive' personal data.

Other things you need to know

- Data in *manual* filing systems is covered by the new Act. However, data in such systems that existed prior to 1 March 1998 does not have to comply with principles 2 to 5 of the Act until October 2007 (so this means that you have until then to get your manual files of personal data cleaned up).
- Previously a data subject could request a copy of the data you hold about him/her. Now the data subject can not only request a copy of everything you hold about them but they can also request a description of the purposes for which the data is held *and* a list of any potential recipients of the data (beware of list swaps!).
- Individuals can insist on having data corrected or erased where appropriate and also insist that you have the data corrected or erased by other organisations you might have sent it to.
- You cannot use the data for direct marketing purposes if the data subject objects. (If an individual requests that you take their name off your database then technically you should do so. However, you might get that individual's name again in a list swap (reciprocal mailing) and this would upset them even more. Instead of deleting the individual from your database you can keep them on file and mark them as 'Never mail – requested deletion'. This procedure has been approved by the Information Commissioner.)
- Individuals can claim compensation for any damage caused by a breach of the Act.

For more about Data Protection, see *Data Protection* by Paul Ticher (details in Appendix One).

Telecommunications

In addition to the Data Protection Act there are the Telecommunications Regulations 1999 (Data Protection and Privacy). These are just as important because they cover charities telephoning (or faxing) people to make appeals for money or other support *and* also just promoting the organisation's aims and ideals. It should be noted that:

- It is a breach of the regulations to telephone someone who has registered with the TPS (Telephone Preference Service).

- It is a breach of the regulations to telephone someone who has previously told you they don't want such calls.

- It is not a breach if you phone someone who has not given you explicit permission to call BUT they have given you their telephone number.

- If you make such a call then the call recipient can request the name and address of the caller or a phone number where you can be reached (and this means you, even if you are having the calls made by an agency on your behalf).

- You must not send unsolicited marketing faxes to individuals without their prior consent.

- You can send marketing faxes to corporate bodies but not if they have registered with the FPS (Fax Preference Service).

Future directions

CHAPTER ELEVEN

Where we are today

This chapter begins by looking at the possibilities for an integrated, organisation-wide database: sharing data without compromising control or security, and tailoring functions to each user or group of users. It moves on to describe some current trends in database development which are designed to increase flexibility and efficiency of database use.

There are an enormous number of contact management/fundraising databases on the market today; at least 80 and probably over 100. They range from the cheap and cheerful to the expensive and sophisticated. No matter what your budget, there is a system you can buy that will probably meet your needs (as long as you tailor your expectations to your budget!). No matter what your needs, there is a system that will probably satisfy at least 90% of them. It is worth remembering that perfection is impossible – the demand for that extra 10% in order to obtain the so-called perfect fit is not worth the huge effort required.

There are systems that do just contact management. There are systems that do contact management and fundraising. There are systems that have sophisticated marketing facilities. There are systems that also do membership and subscriptions. There are systems that do event management. There are systems that do legacy administration, trading/mail order, raffles, payroll giving, matched giving, collection boxes, individual sponsorship, campaign management, fund management, project sponsorship, market research, grant giving, financial assistance, helplines, research grants. There really is something for everyone.

The corporate database

As organisations grow, the number of databases proliferates. In one case a large voluntary organisation counted over 2,000 separate databases amongst it staff. The average is somewhere between 5 and 20. The reasons for such a proliferation are simple:

- Confidentiality – one group in the organisation doesn't want other people messing about with 'their' contacts.

- Speed of implementation – it is quicker and easier to set up a little mailing list in Excel or Access than cooperate with a large corporate project.

- Cost – it is cheaper to do it yourself.

- Ease of use – most people need only a small fraction of the facilities offered by a large database, so their personal database only does the things they want it to.

- Control – if it is on that person's PC then they feel that they have control.

This, however, leads to greater problems:

- No overall view of the whole organisation's communications with a particular contact and who is dealing with whom.

- Different databases with different information, such as different addresses – which one is the latest?

- Several people all doing the same thing, and often in different ways.

- Duplicate mailings and added cost.

- Multiple systems to be supported if something goes wrong.

- Each separate database is likely to be 'owned' and managed by an individual, and if this person leaves or is away for any reason it may be difficult or even impossible to get information out of the system.

The goal of having a single corporate database has long been aimed at. Unfortunately, the theory and the practice have until recently seldom come together. The single corporate database was difficult to implement, took far too long, was very expensive, never satisfied all the users, was impractical for remote users, and cost too much. In particular, it was often found that specialist functions, such as trading/mail order or event management, was not handled at all or was handled poorly by the contact management/fundraising databases. The result in many cases has been the implementation of separate systems. Attempts to integrate these separate systems into a master system providing the definitive source for names and addresses, and subordinate systems that accept changes, have seldom been successful. Systems integration is a complex subject and inevitably involves special programming, thus defeating the purpose of buying a package in the first place.

This situation is changing. Windows based systems, the new breed of object oriented databases and cheap communications via the Internet are combining to turn the dream of a single corporate name and address database, accessible by everyone in the organisation, into reality – and moreover a practical proposition for all organisations, whatever their size and nature.

DATABASE CASE STUDY UNICEF

Background

Since 1993, the UK Committee for Unicef (UKC) had used a fully integrated fundraising, mail order and accounts system. The significant benefits of having full integration from donation processing or order entry through to the management accounts and also to the fundraisers data analysis and segmentations had been experienced. However, the growth potential of the UKC was being severely hampered by the lack of functionality in all the key areas of this system.

In December 1997, the UKC embarked on a thorough look at what form the future database strategy should take to enable us to meet our ambitious growth plans.

Two years later, in December 1999, we went live on Visual Alms. This was after replacing our mail order system and financial systems, also during 1999.

Business Needs Analysis

All UKC staff were involved in establishing our business needs through various dialogues and involving a number of consultants. We conducted a survey through a staff questionnaire and held visionary and ITT definition workshops.

Four key drivers were identified for the UKC database strategy:

- Holistic view – a record of every communication between UKC and the supporter, and also of all the information on each supporter in one place.

- Competitive advantage – open to introducing new initiatives that would need significant ongoing extensions to the functionality of the database.

- Accessible to the fundraiser – in an increasingly sophisticated communication strategy with the supporter, the responsibility of producing necessary data had to shift towards the fundraisers themselves and away from the IT department.

- Best of breed – we believe this would maximise our return on investment, keep the total cost of ownership to a minimum and take full advantage of the experience of others without re-inventing the wheel.

Did we achieve what we set out to do?

The most difficult part of our database strategy to realise has been the holistic view, in light of us making a conscious decision to replace our one integrated system with three separate systems. 18 months down the track, we only have partial integration between mail order and fundraising. There are many pieces in the jigsaw of complete integration, many of which are developed. We just haven't brought them all together and bound them up with a rigorous procedure.

However, what we have been able to do is to deliver on the need of greater sophistication and rolling out the responsibility for many reports and data exports to the fundraisers.

The setting up of a fully integrated Supporter Help Desk within the Visual Alms product has proved our ability to develop the database functionality.

An additional benefit has been the relative ease in which we have automated business processes such as Paperless Direct Debit and Payroll Giving, minimising the need for data processing intervention.

If we had to make the decision again, I can confidently say that we would still choose Visual Alms.

Phil Durbin – Head of IT, Unicef

Some current trends

When considering fundraising databases it is most important to concentrate on the current needs of the organisation and what is available today.

Vapourware

Never buy 'vapourware'. This is software or functions that the salesman says is coming soon. It may never arrive or if it does it will probably be late. Buy on the basis of what you can see working today.

Having said this, it is important to have an eye on the future, particularly in terms of what other organisations are doing or planning to do in the short to medium term. Some database developments that you might not have thought of are being put into practice right now by someone in the voluntary sector. Here is a selection of such current trends.

Computer telephony integration (CTI)

There are two aspects to linking your database to your telephone system.

1 Making outgoing telephone calls. If you store the contact's telephone number it is possible to click a telephone icon, the system dials the contact's number and you pick up the phone when they answer. Combine this with a selection and you can call people one after the other without actually dialling a single number.

2 'Screen popping'. This is applied to incoming telephone calls and is an extension of caller identification which displays the caller's number on a display panel as the telephone rings. In this case the

computer recognises the telephone number and if it is on the database, the fundraising database displays the contact's record for you on the computer screen as you pick up the phone – ideal for helplines.

Multi-media

With more than 50% of homes now having a computer and CD writers becoming very inexpensive, some organisations are sending out CDs as well as or instead of thank-you letters, particularly for the larger donations. A single CD can contain a thank-you message, corporate information such as an annual report, video clips of your project work and appeals for more money.

Voice systems

Voice operated word processing systems have been around for a long time but they have always suffered from taking a long time to 'train' the system, accuracy levels of less than 90% leading to more time spent making corrections than would have been spent typing the information in the first place, and higher cost. Today's voice systems are quick to get started with, can achieve greater than 98% accuracy with sophisticated spelling and grammar checkers and are very inexpensive. Added to that, generalised voice-operated systems are appearing so that all software systems including Windows can be controlled in this way and not just word processing.

Web-enabled databases

With Internet usage continuing to expand at an exponential rate and a trend towards people spending more time working from home, databases are becoming 'web-enabled'. What this means from the fundraiser's point of view is that they can access their database from anywhere in the world and carry out *all* normal functions by connecting to the database over the Internet. This obviates expensive leased lines or dial-up links (which are often poor quality). It is now practical for a regional fundraiser to use the central database from their front room.

DATABASE CASE STUDY
SIGHT SAVERS INTERNATIONAL

There are two core elements to an effective charity fundraising database. Firstly that it's fundamentally sound in terms of the basics such as platform, underlying design, report writers, and accurate administration. Secondly, it has sufficient flexibility to twist and turn and take advantage of new fundraising developments, whether a 'macro' development such as being web-enabled, or a micro-development such as the addition of a new field/column. Unfortunately, it's not always the case that these two core elements are compatible.

However, it's our experience at Sight Savers International that Progress scores highly in both areas and gives us plenty of confidence for the future.

Progress is a relational database sitting on a SQL platform. This means that it's relatively easy for IT to provide the necessary technical and infrastructure support that fundraisers need. Given that in most charities fundraisers and IT are in different departments, with all that this entails, this is important. The main tables are solidly built with all the right keys, and follow the guidebook for good relational database design (such as referential integrity). In particular, the system uses a bridging table between donors and addresses to tackle the problem where a donor can and will have a number of addresses.

The underlying platform supports any number of report writers, such as Crystal, R & R or SQL itself, and report writing is made easier by the underlying logic and common-sense of the table design and fields/columns. In addition to the core tables such as finance, payment plans/commitments, donor details, addresses, contact history, etc., the database also has all the necessary fields to support effective tax reclamation and parameter different rules for the processing of Banked Direct payments. There is also plenty of scope for users to customise the database for their own special requirements, for example, perhaps a special high-value donor scheme, or a complicated set of parameters about 'who should get what' communications. There is also a surprising and unexpected amount of functionality for 'personal sales', which in the charity sector might include Big Gift, Private Appeal, High Value campaigns. It certainly gives Goldmine a run for its money in this area.

However, equally important is that the database is very flexible in terms of being able to allow the users to add new fields, even 'groups', to reflect their ever-changing requirements. Of particular importance in this area is the web. This is not just about storing e-mail addresses, but the ability of the database to generate and fire off e-mail campaigns, to be able to support direct platform interface between the charity's website and its database to avoid 'double-keying', and even a web-enabled version where users (and donors!) can access and amend the database online through the use of a browser. This last-named development should make Progress particularly attractive to charities with strong regional fundraising operations where users are geographically dispersed.

John Lister – Head of Direct Marketing, Sight Savers International

CHAPTER TWELVE

The shrinking world

The final chapter looks at the potential of the Internet, Intranet, and even Extranet, to provide links between data and its users. It also examines how your database system might fit into the wider concept of 'the information society'. A key message of this chapter is the need to utilise what is available and affordable to you now, while realising that as technology improves and changes, you must also keep an eye on the future.

The Internet

The Internet is changing everybody's lives and will continue to do so for the foreseeable future. Your website is your window on the world from which you view the world but through which you too are viewed. The primary use for it is to provide an information resource for people who are surfing the net. With the huge uptake in e-mail, you can keep people in touch with what you are doing on a daily basis if you want to, and a fundraising appeal by e-mail is quick and easy to conduct. The response may be small but then so is the cost.

Many charities are now accepting donations on the Internet. This is done via a link from the charity website to a secure website that can accept credit card details safely (or relatively safely – no system is totally secure, but giving your credit card details on the Internet is no less secure than giving them over the telephone or giving your credit card to a waiter in a restaurant who promptly disappears into the back room with it). These systems can be made to appear seamless to the donor who may think that the payment is going direct to the organisation they are supporting and directly into their database. But this is not so. There is currently no direct link to the fundraising database and the database is updated at a later date either by a file of transactions to be loaded, or more usually, by manually entering the details from a listing provided by the agency collecting the money.

Consequently, by having no direct link with the Internet, the database is secure behind the organisation's firewall software.

The Internet was mentioned above with respect to web-enabled databases. This allows authorised database users (i.e. your staff) to access the database over the Internet and do their work as if they were in the office. The next step is the concept of the 'database-driven website'. You store the details and preferences of the person browsing your website and present them with pages tailored to their activities and interests the next time they visit your site. The information to do this is commonly stored on a separate web database, but it could be stored on the main contacts database where you may already have details of the person including their name and address and probably even their interests as well. From here it is a small step to allow contacts/supporters to access the contacts/fundraising database directly. They would only be allowed to see their own records but they can be encouraged to correct errors and make any other appropriate changes such as change of address and, most importantly, make donations and have them recorded immediately on the database. As we have just discussed, people can already make donations on-line but it is this last part, the immediate link to the fundraising database, that is missing at the present time. This scenario raises huge security issues because supporters of the organisation will be allowed past all the security barriers and into the computer in your office.

The Intranet

Organisations are beginning to implement Intranets, particularly for corporate information like staff handbooks, health and safety regulations, personnel records and the like. It is a short step from here to using a browser interface for accessing all systems including the fundraising database. There would then be one method of accessing data and interacting with systems whether it was on your internal network or external on the World Wide Web.

The Extranet

The Extranet is a name given to linked Intranets such that a person browsing their own corporate computer would be able to link straight through and browse your computer, according to their security clearance of course. A possible scenario could be for you to check on the progress of an application to a charitable trust. You look up the trust on your database, see that the application was lodged four weeks ago, click a link and access the trust's computer and view the application and its status. A potentially somewhat frightening scenario and no-one is doing it yet, but it is only a matter of time. The technology already exists.

The information society

Data warehouses

With the implementation of a modern contact management/fundraising system you could be storing vast amounts of data. This data will consist of support for your organisation both financial and non-financial from thousands of contacts stretching back over many years. This is the beginnings of a data warehouse or more accurately a data mart because it is a single database. A data warehouse consists of a number of databases representing different operational areas of the organisation all brought together into a single relational database so that analysis, manipulation and modelling of different aspects of the business can be considered together. Relationships between seemingly unrelated aspects of the business can be found when the whole organisation is modelled in this way. As organisations store more and more data and the cost of computing continues to fall, such techniques previously reserved for the largest corporate bodies are coming within the reach of voluntary organisations.

Information overload?

The much touted paperless office predicted in the eighties never arrived. What arrived was faster and cheaper printers churning out more and more paper. What also arrived was cheap processing power so more data could be collected and more analysis carried out producing yet more paper. Consider the 125 cells of a three-dimensional recency/frequency/value matrix. Can you actually cope with considering the differences between supporters in each of these cells and treat them individually? Can you reconcile this in your head with scattergrams, chi squared analysis, linear regression and analysis of variance produced by SPSS? Can you overlay it all with fourteen different demographic profiles produced by marketing agencies? Will it all get too much? Luckily, as the ability to produce more analysis increases, so the sophistication of systems to distil the information into manageable chunks increases. These systems are often known as intelligent agents. They work on your behalf sifting vast volumes of information looking for items that are relevant to you and your job. So it never does get too much, the technology changes to keep up with what you can handle.

A plan for the future?

Moore's Law (see page 17) tells us that computer hardware is considered to be out of date in just 18 months. Software systems are out of date in three years. The software you buy today probably won't run on the hardware you bought three years ago. Microsoft Windows is all the rage now but will it still be so in five years time? Will your investment in thousands of pounds worth of cabling for gigabit Ethernet be rendered obsolete by cheap wireless networking in three years time? Will your fundraising database supplier remain in business? Can you predict the future of IT and can you plan for it? The answer is that you cannot see much further than two or three years ahead so don't plan further that that. Buy what is a common standard today and if the situation changes be prepared to change at an appropriate time. But rest assured, if a change is needed there will be many people in the same boat as you and the computer industry will have created the technology required to ease the transition.

The other thing that is certain is that IT (Information Technology) has changed into ICT (Information Communications and Technology) and the focus has changed from a concentration on the technology itself to a concentration on the information that can be obtained from the data in the systems. Hardware is increasingly becoming a commodity item designed to be written off in a single year and operating systems are becoming increasingly easy to use and 'wizard' driven. Fundraising databases are becoming ever more sophisticated but also ever easier (and ever more enjoyable?) to use.

Make the most of and enjoy your database.

Sources of further help

Publications

Building a Fundraising Database using your PC

Peter Flory

DSC in association with CAF

2nd edition 2001

£12.95 ISBN 1 900360 92 6

Data Protection for Voluntary Organisations

Paul Ticher

DSC in association with Bates, Wells & Braithwaite

1st edition 2000

£12.95 ISBN 1 900360 47 0

Data Protection

More information on the Data Protection Act can be obtained from:

Office of the Information Commissioner
Wycliffe House
Water Lane
Wilmslow
Cheshire
SK9 5AF

Tel: 01625 545 700
Website: www.dataprotection.gov.uk

Fundraising software suppliers

The following list of products and their suppliers' addresses is provided for guidance only, and is not intended as an endorsement of any product by either the author or the publisher of this book.

ACORN
(Profiling software)
CACI Limited
CACI House
Avonmore Road
Kensington Village
London
W14 8TS
Tel: 020 7602 6000

Advantage Fundraiser
Redbourn Business Systems Limited
3 Bergham Mews
Blythe Road
London
W14 0HN
Tel: 020 7751 1999

AppealMaster
New Generation Consultancy
Park IT Centre
Coryton
Okehampton
Devon
EX20 4PG
Tel: 01566 783 371

Compton Campaign
Compton International
Compton House
High Street
Harbury
Warwickshire
CV33 9HW
Tel: 01926 614 555

Charisma
Minerva Computer Systems
Ltd
21–22 Imperial Square
Cheltenham
Gloucestershire
GL50 1QZ
Tel: 01242 511 232

CHASql and Fundraiser
AK Consultancies Ltd
141a Prestbury Road
Cheltenham
GL52 2DU
Tel: 01242 234 123

C-MACS
Computer Productivity Ltd
The Belgrade Centre
Denington Road
Wellingborough
Northants
NN8 2QH
Tel: 01933 221 400

Contact Manager
Decisions Express Ltd
Hatherley House
15–17 Wood Street
Barnet
Herts
EN5 4AT
Tel: 020 8441 9800

Contacts Suite
Care Business Solutions Ltd
Ockford Mill
Ockford Road
Godalming
Surrey
GU7 1RH
Tel: 01483 860 001

Donorflex
Care Data Systems
Patrick House
Lakeside Centre
180 Lifford Lane
Kings Norton
Birmingham
B30 3NU
Tel: 0121 458 7887

Enterprise
Accounting Answers Limited
Rumbridge Street
Totton
Southampton
Hampshire
SO40 9DR
Tel: 023 8030 4300

First Class
(Legacy administration)
Clearwater Consultancy Limited
18 St George's Street
Chorley
Lancashire
PR7 2AA
01257 272 730

Genesis
Ramesys
Eldon Way
Crick
Northamptonshire
NN6 7SL
Tel: 01788 822 133

iMembership
Miller Technology
Swinton House
324 Gray's Inn Road
London
WC1X 8DD
Tel: 020 7278 2081

iMIS
Fisher Technology Limited
Acre House
11–15 William Road
London
NW1 3ER
Tel: 020 7388 7000

KISS Contacts
KIS Software Solutions
12A Lypiatt Road
Cheltenham
GL50 2QW
Tel: 01242 262 805

Kubernesis
Kubernesis Partnership
36 Acomb Wood Drive
York
YO2 2XN
Tel: 01904 788 885

Lawbase
(Legacy administration)
Lawbase Legal Systems
Caroline House
55–57 High Holborn
London
WC1V 6DX
Tel: 020 7242 1454

Mailbrain
(Trading/Mail order)
Sanderson IT Systems Ltd
CFL House
Manor Road
Coventry
CV1 2GF
Tel: 024 7655 5466

Mediadisk – see Waymaker Online

MySoft CRM
MySoft ASA
Ole Deviks vei 35
PO Box 6199
Etterstad
0602 Oslo
Norway
Tel: 00 47 23 05 22 00

Open Market
Anglo-Europe Computer Systems Ltd
16–18 King Street
Newcastle-under-Lyme
Staffs
ST5 1ET
Tel: 01782 713 409

Pro2000
Protech Computer Systems Limited
Eldon Court
Eldon Street
Walsall
West Midlands
WS1 2JP
Tel: 01922 722 280

Proclaim
Avant-Garde Software Solutions Ltd
Charter House
51–53 Bickersteth Road
London
SW17 9SH
Tel: 020 8672 2808

Progress
Fisk Brett Ltd
Olivier House
High Street
Steyning
West Sussex
BN44 3RE
Tel: 01903 879 379

Raiser's Edge
Blackbaud Europe Ltd
112 Cornwall Street South
Glasgow
G41 1AA
Tel: 0141 575 0000

RealAppeal
Charity Communications
Glebe House
St Michaels
Tenbury Wells
WR15 8PH
Tel: 01584 810 512

SPSS
(Statistical analysis
software)
SPSS UK Ltd
St. Andrew's House
West Street
Woking
Surrey
GU21 1FY

Stratum
APT Solutions Limited
Business Design Centre
52 Upper Street
London
N1 0QH
Tel: 020 7704 8006

Subscriber
Dataware Consultancy
Centre Ltd
25 Northfields
Grays
Essex
RM17 5TN
Tel: 01375 383 874

Target
Centrepoint Computer
Services Limited
Tolworth Tower
Ewell Road
Surbiton
Surrey
KT6 7EL
Tel: 020 8390 8899

thankQ
ESIT Limited
Loughborough Technology Centre
Epinal Way
Loughborough
Leicestershire
LE11 3GE
Tel: 01509 235 544

Visible Results
SunDayta Ltd
27 Herrick Close
Crawley
West Sussex
RH10 3AN
Tel: 01293 407 474

Visual Alms
Westwood Forster Limited
13–27 Brunswick Place
London
N1 6DX
Tel: 020 7251 4890

Waymaker Online
(incorporating **Mediadisk**)
(Media Contacts)
Waymaker
Chess House
34 Germain Street
Chesham
Bucks
Tel: 01494 797 225

Postcode software suppliers

Software suppliers who provide systems that utilise the Royal mail's
Postcode Address File (PAF) include:

AFD Postcode
AFD Software Ltd
Old Post Office Lane
West Quay
Ramsey
Isle of Man
IM8 1RF
Tel: 01624 811 711

GB Mailing
GB Mailing Systems Limited
Winster House
Herons Way
Chester Business Park
Chester
CH4 9QR

Hopewiser
187 Hale Road
Hale
Altrincham
WA15 8DG
Tel: 0161 941 6111

QAS Systems Ltd
(Quick Address)
7 Old Town
London
SW4 0YY
Tel: 020 7498 7777

Preference Services

These services are provided by the Direct Marketing Association.

Mailing Preference Service
Freepost 22
London
W1E 7EZ
Tel: 020 7766 4410
e-mail: mps@dma.org.uk

Telephone Preference Service
5th floor
Haymarket House
1 Oxendon Street
London
SW1Y 4EE
Tel: 020 7766 4420
e-mail: tps@dma.org.uk

Fax Preference Service
5th floor
Haymarket House
1 Oxendon Street
London
SW1Y 4EE
Tel: 020 7766 4422
e-mail: fps@dma.org.uk

Glossary

ASCII (American Standard Code for Information Interchange) The most common format for defining characters that is universally recognised by all makes of computer.

ASP (Application Service Provider) A company that operates and manages your software application (in this case a fundraising database) on their own computers and you access the application via telephone connections.

batch processing Processing a number of transactions at the same time usually with control procedures to ensure that all items are processed accurately.

Boolean logic Complex expressions using combinations of logical operators ('and', 'or' and 'not'), mathematical and text operators and brackets.

browser interface With respect to fundraising databases this refers to using the same facilities that you use to access and use the Internet to access and use the database.

concurrent users The number of users actually using the database at any one instant in time. (Note that this includes users who have the database open but who are not actually doing anything with it.)

CSV (Comma Separated Values) The most common format for defining a file of information to be exchanged between computers, where the individual fields are separated by commas.

database A collection of related information.

Database Management System (DBMS) A suite of computer programs that provide facilities to manage a database. These programs control the organisation, storage, retrieval, security and integrity of the data held within the database.

export The act of taking data out of your database in order to use it in another system, such as in an Excel spreadsheet.

Extranet Linked Intranets – browsing your own internal Intranet can take you seamlessly through to another organisation's Intranet.

field An individual item of data which may be contained in a column of a database table, for example town, county or postcode.

file A related set of records, such as a file of name and address records.

folder Synonymous with file. One of many terms introduced with Windows-type computer systems to make the computer more user-friendly.

Gb (Gigabyte) One billion characters of information.

icon A picture to represent a computer program or function instead of words.

import The act of bringing data into your database from another computerised source, for instance from an Excel spreadsheet.

indexed fields A technical facility applied to data fields that you use to search for individual records most often, e.g. postcode or surname, so that the required record can be found very quickly without the system having to search the whole database for it.

Internet A world-wide link-up of computer networks which allows the exchange of information in a common format.

Intranet An implementation of facilities within your own organisation accessed by a standard web browser.

iterative selections Selections within other selections which continually narrow down the number of records being searched.

K (Kb – Kilobyte) One thousand characters of information.

keyed fields See indexed fields.

LAN (Local Area Network) A network of local computers, typically in the same building.

Mailsort order Pre-sorting mailings into a sequence defined by the Post Office (in order to make their job easier) that earns the customer significant postage discounts (only for mailings in excess of 4,000 items).

Mb (Megabyte) One million characters of information.

module A group of computer programs that all belong to a single overall function, such as Mail Order or Event Management (often priced and sold separately by the database suppliers).

network Two or more computers connected together so that they can exchange information.

outsourcing The process of getting an external agency to manage a complete application (see ASP).

PAF (Postcode Address File) A computer file containing the details of every postal address in the UK produced and regularly updated by the Royal Mail.

Pareto analysis The 80:20 rule – 80% of your income comes from 20% of your donors. (Named after an eighteenth century French/Italian economist.)

postcode software Computer systems that use the PAF to provide the user with facilities such as displaying the entire address when the user enters the postcode.

profiling The process of coding the records on the database according to similar characteristics usually based on postcode, for example CACI's ACORN code.

RAM (Random Access Memory) Computer memory that you can read from and write to.

record A set of related data items or fields.

relational database A collection of related information that is organised as a table or as a series of related tables.

RFV (Recency/Frequency/Value) analysis Recency – how long since the donor last gave;
Frequency – how often has the donor given;
Value – how much has the donor given.
(Sometimes known as RFM – Recency, Frequency, Monetary value.)

ROM (Read Only Memory) Computer memory that you can read but cannot alter.

segmentation The process of splitting the supporters on your database into groups with similar attributes, for example all those who give by cheque and who haven't given so far this year.

selection criteria Characteristics of a supporter, which can be used to choose people of a similar type. For example, if you want to print a list of all people who have given more than £100 in the last two years then your selection criteria are 'total gifts greater than £100' and 'every gift where the gift date is greater than the date two years ago'.

soft credit The action of entering a money value which can be displayed and reported on but which is not included in any financial totals, for example a gift membership where a 'real' credit is applied to the person paying the membership and a 'soft' credit is applied to the person whose membership it is paying for.

spreadsheet A page of tables (columns and rows) of data, usually numeric, that can be manipulated by a computer program such as Excel.

stand-alone A term used for a computer that is not connected to any other computer.

subfolder A sub-set of records from a folder, such as only the names and addresses of our corporate contacts.

suppression file A file of names and addresses that can be compared against a mailing list so that any names appearing on it (the suppression file) are removed from the mailing, for example a file of deceased people.

Unique Reference Number (URN) A shorthand way of referencing people by allocating them a number which is unique to them.

About the Directory of Social Change

The Directory of Social Change (DSC) is an independent voice for positive social change, set up in 1975 to help voluntary organisations become more effective. It does this by providing practical, challenging and affordable information and training to meet the current, emerging and future needs of the sector.

DSC's main activities include:

- researching and publishing reference guides and handbooks;
- providing practical training courses;
- running conferences and briefing sessions;
- organising Charityfair, the biggest annual forum for the sector;
- encouraging voluntary groups to network and share information;
- campaigning to promote the interests of the voluntary sector as a whole.

The Directory of Social Change

24 Stephenson Way
London
NW1 2DP

Federation House
Hope Street
Liverpool
L1 9BW

Publications and subscriptions
tel: 020 7209 5151
fax: 020 7209 5049

Publicity and research
tel: 020 7209 4422
0151 708 0136

Courses and conferences
tel: 020 7209 4949
0151 708 0117

Charityfair
tel: 020 7209 4949
020 7209 1015 (exhibitors)

website: www.dsc.org.uk
e-mail: info@dsc.org.uk

Other publications from the Directory of Social Change

All the following titles are published by the Directory of Social Change, unless otherwise stated, and are available from:

Publications Department
Directory of Social Change
24 Stephenson Way
London
NW1 2DP

Call 020 7209 5151 or e-mail info@dsc.org.uk for more details and for a free publications list, which can also be viewed at the DSC website (www.dsc.org.uk).

Prices were correct at the time of going to press but may be subject to change.

The fundraising series
Published in association with CAF and ICFM

Community Fundraising

Harry Brown

Volunteer networks are a key resource for fundraising, but are often not appreciated as they should be. This book demonstrates how to make the most of your volunteers. It covers:

- what community fundraising is
- why people volunteer, the value of volunteers and staff attitudes to volunteers
- the recruitment, retention and development of volunteers
- the management of staff working with volunteers
- case studies from a range of different types of charities – and what can be learned from these.

Corporate Fundraising

Edited by Valerie Morton

This book provides a comprehensive overview of corporate fundraising, detailing the variety of ways in which charities and companies may work together to mutual advantage. A broad selection of case studies illustrates the topics discussed, including some of the ethical issues raised by such partnerships.

176 pages, 1st edition, 1999 ISBN 1 85934 057 1 £19.95

Fundraising Strategy

Redmond Mullin

Rigorous strategic planning is a prerequisite of a successful fundraising campaign. In this accessible guide the author, a recognised expert in the field of fundraising, aims to clarify the principle and process of strategy and to demonstrate its place in fundraising campaigns by:

- discussing the concept of strategy and its relevance for not-for-profit bodies;
- outlining the planning process for designing and implementing the strategy behind the campaign;
- providing case studies of different strategies in different types and sizes of funding programmes.

152 pages, 1st edition, 1997 ISBN 1 85934 056 3 £14.95

Trust Fundraising

Edited by Anthony Clay

This book outlines a variety of approaches to trusts that will save trustees' time and ensure greater success for fundraising by:

- emphasising the importance of research and maintaining records;
- demonstrating the value of using contacts and a personal approach;
- reinforcing the need for detailed planning of a strategy;
- showing how to make an approach to trusts, and how not to;
- stressing the importance of continued contact with a trust.

152 pages, 1st edition, 1999 ISBN 1 85934 069 5 £19.95

Legacy Fundraising

Edited by Sebastian Wilberforce

This unique guide to one of the most important sources of revenue for charities has been revised and updated to include new material on telephone fundraising, forecasting income, and profiling. It also contains the full text of the new ICFM Code of Practice on legacy fundraising. Contributions from a range of experts in the field cover both strategy and techniques, and are complemented by perspectives from donors and their families. The breadth of coverage and accessible style ensure that, whether you are an established legacy fundraiser or new to the field, this book is a must.

224 pages, 2nd edition, 2001
ISBN 1 900360 93 4 £19.95

Other titles from DSC

The Complete Fundraising Handbook

Nina Botting & Michael Norton
Published in association with ICFM

For the new edition of this ever-popular title, the information has been completely updated and also reorganised, making it even easier to use. It is now divided into three parts, covering:

- fundraising principles and strategies;
- sources of fundraising – including individual donors, grant-making trusts, companies, central and local government;
- fundraising techniques – from house-to-house collections and challenge events, to direct mail and capital appeals.

Illustrated with case studies throughout, the book provides a wealth of practical advice on every aspect of fundraising for charity.

368 pages, 4th edition, 2001   ISBN 1 900360 84 5   £16.95

The Grant-making Trusts CD-ROM

Software development by Funderfinder
Published in association with CAF

This CD-ROM combines the trusts databases of the Directory of Social Change and the Charities Aid Foundation to provide the most comprehensive and up-to-date information ever on grant-making trusts. It contains details of all trusts as listed in the *Directory of Grant Making Trusts*, the three *Guides to Major Trusts*, the *Guide to Scottish Trusts*, and the four *Guides to Local Trusts*.

- Total of nearly 4,000 trusts.
- Network capability.
- Hyperlinks to trust websites or email.
- Improved search facilities, including search by trustee name.
- Runs on Windows 95/98, 2000, NT and Millennium.

Single CD-ROM, 1st edition, 2001

ISBN 1 900360 94 2 £110 + VAT = £129.25

£80 + VAT = £94 for existing users of the CD-ROM *Trusts Guide* or *Grantseeker* CD-ROM.

About CAF

CAF, Charities Aid Foundation, is a registered charity with a unique mission – to increase the substance of charity in the UK and overseas. It provides services that are both charitable and financial which help donors make the most of their giving and charities make the most of their resources.

As an integral part of its activities, CAF works to raise standards of management in voluntary organisations. This includes the making of grants by its own Grants Council, sponsorship of the Charity Annual Report and Accounts Awards, seminars, training courses and its own Annual Conference, the largest regular gathering of key people from within the voluntary sector. In addition, CAF is recognised as a leading exponent of the internet for all those with an interest in charitable activity.

For decades, CAF has led the way in developing tax-effective services to donors, and these are now used by more than 250,000 individuals and 2,000 of the UK's leading companies, between them giving £150 million each year to charity. Many are also using CAF's CharityCard, the world's first debit card designed exclusively for charitable giving. CAF's unique range of investment and administration services for charities includes the CafCash High Interest Cheque Account, three specialist investment funds for longer-term investment and a full appeals and subscription management service.

CAF's activities are not limited to the UK, however. Increasingly, CAF is looking to apply the same principles and develop similar services internationally, in its drive to increase the substance of charity across the world. CAF has offices and sister organisations in the United States, Bulgaria, South Africa, Russia, India and Brussels.

CAF Research is a leading source of information and research on the voluntary sector's income and resources. Its annual publication, *Dimensions of the Voluntary Sector*, provides year-on-year updates and its Research Report series covers a wide range of topics, including costs benchmarking, partnership resources, and trust and company funding. More details on research and publications may be found on www.CAFonline.org/research

For more information about CAF, please visit www.CAFonline.org/

About ICFM

The Institute of Charity Fundraising Managers (ICFM) is the only organisation that exists to represent and support the professional interests of fundraisers at all levels. ICFM welcomes membership applications from all those working in a fundraising role or consultancy practice – from those new to the profession to those with many years' experience.

The benefits to be gained are available to all. As a professional body, ICFM assists its members at every stage and in every facet of their professional development. It provides opportunities for continuing professional education, a forum for discussion on issues of common concern, a source of information and a point of contact with other professionals.

The ICFM Certificate of Membership is evidence of the holder's commitment to the Codes and the professional standards set by the Institute. Since membership is individual, it is fully transferable if you change your job. In liaison with other umbrella groups, ICFM also represents members' interests to charities, government, the media and to the public.

ICFM is supported financially by many charities who recognise the importance and needs of the organisation, having become affiliates of its Charitable Trust. Fundraising staff of these affiliated charities enjoy reduced subscription fees. Through its members, ICFM liaises worldwide with allied organisations, such as the National Society of Fundraising Executives in the USA and the Australian Institute of Fundraising, and is represented on the World Fundraising Council.

ICFM aims, through its Trust, to further knowledge, skills and effectiveness in the field of fundraising. It serves the interests of its members, the professional fundraisers, and through them, the interests of charitable bodies and donors. ICFM aims to set and develop standards of fundraising practice which encompass:

- growth in the funds and resources available for charitable expenditure;
- thorough knowledge of proven fundraising techniques;
- new fundraising opportunities;
- cost effectiveness;
- strict adherence to the law;
- accountability.

ICFM Codes of Practice, Guidance Notes, and the Charity Donors' Rights Charter

The ICFM Codes of Practice and Guidance Notes aim to act as a guide to best practice for fundraisers, and as a benchmark against which the public can measure fundraising practice. They cover a wide variety of issues and aim to address both practical and ethical concerns.

The Codes are drawn up by working parties composed of representatives of the various interested constituents in a particular field, and undergo an extensive consultation process through the charities affiliated to the ICFM, regulators and government.

As new areas of interest are identified, so new Codes are drafted, often at the rate of two or three each year, under the supervision of the ICFM's Standards Committee. Both Charity Commission and Home Office are represented on this committee and play a major role in the development of any new work.

The Codes are endorsed and observed by fundraising organisations throughout the UK. They are recognised as demonstrating the commitment of the voluntary sector to the promotion of best practice.

The Charity Donors' Rights Charter has been developed as a compact between fundraisers and the supporters of the organisations for which they work. It aims to address the expectations that a supporter has of the organisation they give to, and to articulate the commitment the sector makes to them.

Codes of Practice

Charity Challenge Events
UK Charity Challenge Events
Fundraising in Schools
House to House Collections
Telephone Recruitment of Collectors
Personal Solicitation of Committed Gifts
Legacy Fundraising

Outbound Telephone Support
Payroll Giving
Reciprocal Charity Mailings

Guidance Notes

The Acceptance and Refusal of Donations
Data Protection Act 1998
The Management of Static Collection Boxes
The Use of Chain Letters as a Fundraising Technique
UK Charity Challenge Events

New Codes for 2001

Raffles and Lotteries
Fundraising on the Internet

Copies of the Codes of Practice, Guidance Notes and Charity Donors'
Rights Charter may be obtained from ICFM at:

ICFM
5th Floor
Market Towers
1 Nine Elms Lane
London SW8 5NQ

Tel: 020 7627 3436

Or from:
enquiries@icfm.co.uk

Index